From Success to Significance: The Radical CPA Guide
Strategies, Tools & Stories

By Jody Padar, CPA

Advance Praise for
From Success to Significance: The Radical CPA Guide

"Bold and courageous describes Jody Padar's many powerful ideas that all CPA firm leaders must now embrace to build significant and iconic organizations that attract great clients, great employees and great partners. With this book, Jody changes your thinking and gives you the technological processes and culture changing actions to create a fun, productive, enviable and very profitable organization. The most fatal mistake would be for you and your partners to not reread From Success to Significance numerous times to internalize its raw power, honesty, and magic."
   Tony Batman, Chairman and CEO, 1st Global Research & Consulting

"Forget everything you have heard about the future of accounting and read this book. I wish I had this book three years ago instead of having to work all this out myself. Jody Padar is bold in telling us what needs to change, but she has done it, so we should listen. This is a must read, very seriously."
   David Boyar, Chief Executive Officer, Sequel CFO

"Jody does an admirable job of challenging many of the legacy beliefs and processes that limit CPA firms' ability to be truly innovative today. If you intentionally look for things to challenge your present beliefs, you can't read this book without finding a nugget or two to #beEvenBetter."
   Joey Havens, CPA, CGMA, Executive Partner, Horne LLP

"The idea of an agile accounting firm is both surprising and ingenious. That Jody's using what she's learned from engaging with companies in Silicon Valley to rethink the business of accounting is as exciting to me as it is obvious to her."
   James Helms, Vice President, Design Intuit

"You might have heard the saying, 'What got us here, won't get us there.' This could not be more true than today. We are truly in the midst of a strategic inflection point in this profession driven by the hard trends of exponential technologies and demographics. What is needed is a way to see though this fog of uncertainty and ways to leverage the exciting opportunities ahead of us. Jody Padar has been on the edge of this movement and this book offers a roadmap to help you see the exciting possibilities and dare I say 'anticipate' an exciting future for your firm. #futureready"

Tom Hood, CPA, CITP, CGMA and CEO of the Maryland Association of CPAs and the Business Learning Institute

"Jody is correct when she implores: 'CPAs, it's up to you to lead in your firms.' To become a viable firm in the future will require a new type of leadership. It's no longer a matter of managing hourly billing rates, chargeable hours, and realization percentages. Instead, CPA leaders must develop a new mindset and skills in strategic thinking, disruption, innovation, digital transformation, talent development, and customer intimacy. From Success to Significance jump-starts the conversation and provides a helpful roadmap for the CPA who wants to thrive, not just survive, in this rapidly changing marketplace."

Jon Lokhorst, CEO, Lokhorst Consulting LLC

"Jody powerfully reminds us that CPA firms of today cannot meet the complex and demanding needs of their customers tomorrow unless they challenge themselves to break free of their status quo. In this powerful follow up to her first book, Jody continues what makes her so admirable: she challenges us to become RADICAL: to think differently, act differently, serve differently, and grow differently. In this book, Jody gives CPA firms a must-read roadmap for developing the firm of the future, whether you are reengineering a multi-generational firm or beginning a start-up, whether you are a sole practitioner or part of a multi-hundred partner team. Read this book, you and your firm will be better for it!"

David Knoch, President, 1st Global Research & Consulting

"This book, in my opinion, is required reading for everyone that runs an accounting practice or wants to run one, or who is a user of accounting services. It is actually three books with one title and under one cover. It is a book on client services and engagement management; a book on managing staff with self-empowerment; and an unbelievably great book on IT resources available to accounting firms and for their clients—unbelievably great! There are many threads throughout the book—many of which Jody is known for—that provide great guidance, advice, and insights on the 'new way' of delivering client services. Some of her ideas are radical, but not to her and hundreds of firms that are already using these methods, and is a must read, if for no other reason than to gain an understanding of a new model of client engagement, transferring value, and pricing services. Clients should read it to get a glimpse of the essence of how they can benefit from their collaboration with their accounting firms. Jody did good and I highly recommend this book."
   Edward Mendlowitz, CPA, Partner, WithumSmith+Brown, PC

"The accounting profession is changing at an astronomical pace, and Jody Padar is in the engine room. This book is a must for any accountant that wants to lead their firm into the 21st century."
   Chris Hooper, CEO, Accodex

"The most important thing I am reminded of every time I talk to Jody or read her books is to never stay still, to always keep moving forward. That as good as today is, there is never a doubt that we have the power to make a better tomorrow—if we take action."
   Nate Biddick, Assistant Vice President, Consulting - 1st Global

"In her first book, Jody introduced the Radical CPA. In this second, book, she shows us how to put the Radical in CPA. She gives us five basic tenets to future-proof our firms, and gives us the visions and tools to be truly Radical."
   Frank Stitely, CPA, CVA, Managing Member / Partner, Stitely & Karstetter, PLLC

"Jody is a very forward-thinking person. She was among those ahead of the curve in recognizing that we are way past the days where the numbers being "right" is enough. People today crave insight from those numbers. Through today's (and tomorrow's) technological innovations, CPAs are better positioned than ever to turn those numbers into actionable tasks for your clients. In Jody, you could not find a better mentor to help you realize how to use technology in a way that brings real value, to both your firm and your clients. Jody was cloud BEFORE cloud was cool!"
Ronald Thomas, Sr. Trainer, Learning & Development, Sage

"Innovation is not a part of anyone's job description in most CPA firms, but it should be part of regular firm operations with Jody's concept of every day innovation. It doesn't matter the size of your firm; this book provides solid advice and insightful examples to show how you can work to innovate and improve every aspect of your business. If you are brave enough to be radical and lead your firm into its next evolution, start with this book."
Katie Tolin, President, CPA Growth Guides

Copyright © 2017 by Jody Padar. All rights reserved.

Published by CPA Trendlines, an imprint of Bay Street Group LLC, East Hampton, NY, USA, which is the sole owner of exclusive rights of the work in all media and forms and the authorized agent of the author in all matters pertaining to the work.

No part of this publication may be reproduced, stored in a retrieval system, or transmitted in any form or by any means, electronic, mechanical, photocopying, recording, scanning, or otherwise, except as permitted under Section 107 or 108 of the 1976 United States Copyright Act, without prior written permission of the publisher. Such requests should be addressed: Permissions, CPA Trendlines, PO 5139, East Hampton, NY 11937, USA, or via permissions@cpatrendlines.com

Disclaimer: The publisher and the author have used their best efforts in preparing this publication and make no representations or warranties with respect to the accuracy or completeness of the content and specifically disclaim any implied warranties or merchantability or fitness for a particular purpose. No warranty may be created or extended by sales representatives or written materials. The advice contained herein may not be applicable to your situation. You should consult with a professional where appropriate. Neither the publisher nor author shall be liable for any loss or profit or any commercial damages, including but not limited to special, incidental, consequential or other damages. All product names, logos, and brands are property of their respective owners. All company, product and service names used are for identification purposes only. Use of these names, logos, and brands does not necessarily imply endorsement.

Library Data
Padar, Jody

ISBN-13: 978-0999035696
ISBN-10: 099903569X

Book design by DittoDoesDesign.com

For Nicole

"*A hero is an ordinary individual who finds strength to persevere and endure in spite of overwhelming obstacles.*"
—*Christopher Reeve*

Bonus Downloadable Files

Note: Many of the tables, checklists, and worksheets in this handbook are available for download as customizable files at:

https://cpatrendlines.com/radical-cpa-guide-bonus/

Contents

Introduction: How Did We Get Here & Where Are We Going? 1

Chapter 1: The Radical Road to (Business) Transformation 17

Chapter 2: Dear Midsized Firms (Yes, You Can Change) 27

Chapter 3: Firm Product Management is the Way to the Future 55

Chapter 4: Embrace Difference & Diversity 91

Chapter 5: Technology + Transparency = Transformation 113

Chapter 6: Maximizing Social Media and Product Marketing & the Importance of People 125

Chapter 7: Name Your Price 129

Chapter 8: Join the Radical Movement 153

INTRODUCTION

How Did We Get Here & Where Are We Going?

The Radical CPA: Always Changing

People always ask me why Radical? Isn't it a charged word?

What's so Radical about me?

When I talk about Radical, it's not so much about me, but about my beliefs and actions.

Being Radical means being different from what is traditional or ordinary or average.

It's that basic. And it's that important.

And yes, it's about having an extreme political or social view that's not shared by most people. But that's not why I adopted the word.

Seven years ago, when The Radical CPA was born, I was the weirdo accountant. I was totally the odd woman out.

But the world has changed (I say this a lot). And if you've read my first book, you're aware of how much.

Now, the accounting industry needle has moved. The original Radical CPA movement, which included Shayna Chapman, Jason Blumer, W. Michael Hsu, and Chris Farmand started something.

And I'm proud to say, more CPAs have continued to come along.

Being Radical might in fact be more common now than ever before, but we're still on the fringe, growing. Radicals make up about five percent of the accounting population now. There are still many firms who look at us and exclaim, "Wow, I can't believe firms do stuff like that!"

We Want You to Join Us

Perhaps the backbone of our mission is too simple, but we're changing because our customers in the world around us are changing. (Get used to it, this is my mantra.)

It just comes down to that. And because we've been adaptable, we've thrived.

We're not changing because we necessarily wanted to change; we're changing because it's necessary.

It's our reality.

We want to share what we're seeing and learning. That's what The Radical CPA movement is about. We're about getting everybody Radicalized. I want to share with you what I've learned, and I want you think about how to change your firm. The future of our profession relies on us becoming more creative and relevant—working smarter, not harder.

A New Business Model For the New Firm

What if there were a practical way to evolve, change, innovate and, yes, totally restructure your firm as you know it today? A way to fully embody the Radical CPA tenets (and their evolution), and learn how to move with the fast-paced demands of your customers and technology?

This book will serve as your roadmap on how to recreate your business model. Love them or hate them, a business model is a necessary tool, a compass, if you will, on how to focus your business. It's a living, breathing document, but the key is, that it exists. This book is more than a checklist. This is where goals are defined and initiatives are completed despite the intense demand of your workload. This is where extra capacity is found, firm goals are shared, and all the related parties understand priorities and possibilities. This is Business School 101 for the New Firm. A practical, hands-on approach to a CPA firm that will thrive in the future.

This system will give you the tools and resources needed to Radicalize your firm. It will allow you to start big or small. It can move a large firm, a mid-sized firm, or even a firm of one.

Do you know where you want your roadmap to go? A glimpse at the New Vision CPA Group roadmap.

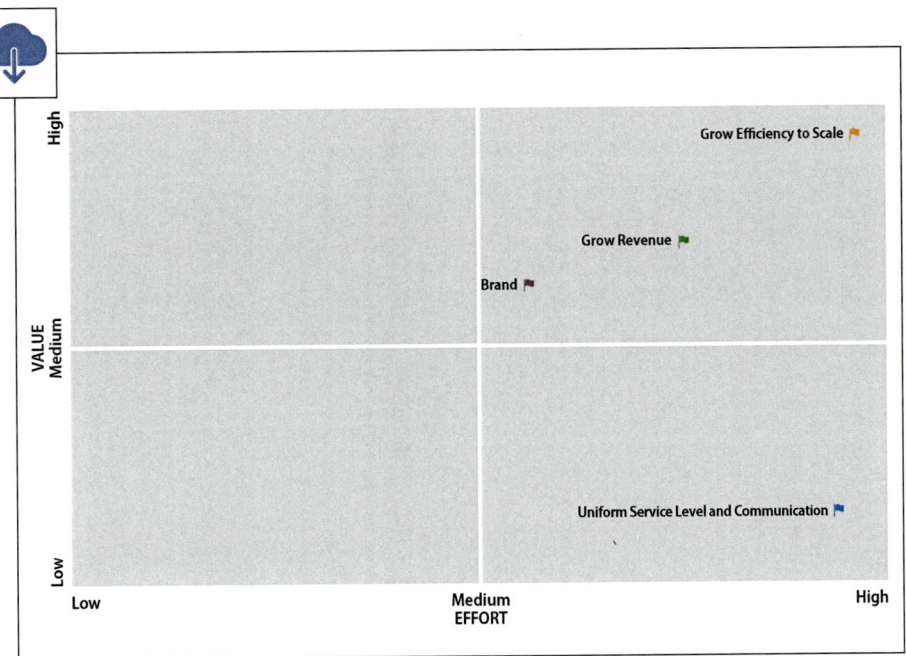

New Vision's Big Picture Goals

At the highest level, it begins with a simple defining of goals that are important to your firm. The above chart is my top-of-mind picture to remind me and my firm what's important. This is what our firm works toward every day, and everyone knows it.

New Vision's Top-Level Initiatives

The above are the initiatives that help New Vision achieve our four goals. They begin to give us boundaries and structure to allow us to implement our bigger goals.

And so begins our roadmap. Keep the visual in mind as you read through the book so you can begin to develop yours.

The Four Tenets: A Brief Review

Before we can fully leap into the future, we need to understand where we've been. The foundation of any Radical or New Firm is comprised of the four tenets.

What are the tenets of a Radical firm?

In my first book, *The Radical CPA: New Rules for a Future-Ready Firm*, I identified four tenets that make up the New Firm of today: cloud technology, social business, value pricing, and customer experiential process. How you apply these tenets will depend on your firm's lifecycle and specific niche and specialty. Application will vary.

The beautiful thing about these tenets—and I've seen this in my work with other CPAs—is they will help you create new rules for your firm. These new rules, practices, and behaviors will make you future-ready. Say goodbye to change management. Creativity and innovation are now part of your DNA. It starts to envelop your whole firm, and everyone becomes part of it. Those who don't come with you will need to be let go—no matter if he is a customer or an employee. You're no longer catching up, and you're no longer constantly trying to respond to one specific change, because it's just ongoing. Let me repeat: There is no end to the change! The benefits to running your business this way, believe me, are exponential.

Transitioning to a Radical firm: Bringing a Legacy Customer Along

As you migrate your firm's current customer base to your new way of working, you may be surprised by how your customers will adapt.

Many of my small business customers are near world-famous locations.

You may have heard of or seen the first season of the hit Netflix series, "Making a Murderer."

The murder took place outside of Sheboygan, Wisconsin, at a junkyard.

It's kind of in the middle of nowhere.

Around the time I got hooked on that series, we were visiting a customer in Kewaunee, which is within 10 minutes of where the murder took place.

Our customer, John, is an interesting and colorful character.

John happens to be in the business of hauling trash and recycling—but he's not connected to the junkyard in the show.

He talks about the "goat farm"—the waste management facility—and needing to take the "goats"—the recycling bins—to the goat farm.

He's in the business of doing a lot of things.

If he sees an opportunity to make money, that's the business he's in. Maybe you have a customer like him.

He also sells, repairs, and stores boats.

The relationship with this customer began when my dad purchased his boat from him in 1996 or so.

They got to talking, and like any good rainmaking partner, it went from buying a boat to gaining a customer.

The "goat farm" is a traditional old-school customer, and in the early days of the relationship, my dad would stop on the way to the lake house to check in with John.

He was an annual tax customer. As we transitioned our firm and changed our customer experience, we transitioned them to quarterly check-ins with value pricing, moved their data from a desktop to the cloud, and connected on social media.

John is in his mid-fifties and has been in business for a very long time.

Let's just call him established.

He doesn't fit the profile of many of our other customers.

However, he trusted us to lead him to where he needed to be for the future of his business.

He gets a lot of business from the people who own summer homes in the area.

They come from major metropolitan areas, and are accustomed to doing business through technology. Being completely automated has been important to his customers and his staff . . . okay . . . his wife, Lynn.

She does all the administrative work, and the transition has made her job easier. Happy wife, happy life. Right?

Anyhow, moving to the cloud provided her with support she didn't have before, even though she didn't change accounting firms.

We could see the same data she was viewing, because it was real-time.

We could be more responsive, because we had better access than when we were emailing data files or "remoting in" to transfer updated data.

We transitioned them slowly, starting with payroll.

When they became comfortable with that, we started remoting in.

Then, they were ready to be fully in the cloud.

We went to Kewaunee for a succession planning meeting.

While we were there, we talked about the show and he told us how close we were to the junkyard.

He gave us directions and I told him we were going to go take a selfie at the sign and post it on Facebook.

John said, "Oh, I didn't know you were on Facebook!" I chuckled to myself, because even my mother is on Facebook!

John gave us directions and asked if I would share the photo with him.

I think as soon as we got in the car, John sent me a friend request—and I shared the photo.

Since then, I've gotten to know John so much better.

I know about what he thinks about GMOs, being an active Lions member, what he's looking for in a feed manager for his daughter's calf farm, that he sells animal bedding, that he has dumpsters available for people who need them after a big storm, and that you can get discounted boat storage if you get your boat in early—and we're his accountants!

In addition, John often sends emails that reference my social media activity.

It has allowed him to know me better, too.

He's obviously reading my posts, which means he's also getting the value-added information I share about taxes.

In addition, he uses the private message feature to ask questions about actual business-related matters.

The virtual relationship has made for a stronger business relationship.

Because we are now working in real-time, they are enjoying a better customer experience. We're not sending large data files back and forth with the potential for either us or them using the wrong version of the file.

We can be more responsive when we get an email or private message on Facebook.

They also don't have to wait until we're making a trip up north to have a conversation.

Because we're handling all the business transactions as they happen, it's more of a social call than a business meeting when we stop in Kewaunee.

He usually has a special bottle of wine for me.

In terms of pricing, moving them to the cloud increased their annual expenditure with us. Because of the value they receive, there was no pushback on the price.

Before we transitioned them, calling us was a stressor for Lynn.

Because of the nature of how John does business, there are complex transactions, and she was on her own in making the appropriate entries.

We often had to correct entries at the end of the year.

It was hard to get to the detail of what the transaction was and why it was entered the way it was.

Now, she knows she can call anytime with a question—without being charged—and we can immediately access their data to make sure entries are made properly.

For instance, they seem to have drivers who total a truck at least once a year.

If you're spending that much time on the road, I guess it's bound to happen.

They get an insurance payment and need to buy a new truck, so they must swap out loans.

Today, Lynn calls us and we record the transaction for her.

It's quick and it's a lot less painful for Lynn and, ultimately, for us, too.

That's the value in value pricing.

And, by the way, John has a brother, Paul, with a lighting store in Green Bay, Wisconsin, and because of John's referral, he is now our customer, also.

So, the four tenets. They are foundational. Understand them first. Without them you're not really a New Firm. But this is The Radical CPA 2.0, right? We've evolved and the tenets have evolved with us.

Tenet #1: Cloud Technology

We all know technology has leveled the playing field. Just mere years ago, bigger firms with sophisticated resources had the upper hand and competitive advantage. Today, because of the genius of the cloud, that has changed. My firm, New Vision CPA Group, comprises only five people, yet, we're regularly competing with firms on a global and national level. Our nimbleness allows us to compete faster because it's harder for the bigger firms to move.

I'm convinced this is because we use technology at our core. Video meetings have changed the nature of how we work. It doesn't matter if our customer is in Los Angeles or Rome. With a strong, reliable Internet connection, we can be screen-sharing and talking about financial statements with our customers within minutes. Anywhere in the world.

I love technology, and, at my firm, we swear by it every day. But I'm the first to say, that's not what it's all about. Technology is a tool. What's at our core as CPAs is practice management. It's about how I run my firm. I've seen too many people get focused on the widgets of technology and the shininess and coolness factors. That's good and all, but what I want to know is, what is it going to do for your firm, and, more importantly, your customers?

Be somewhat choosy here. Step back and think about what the technology is doing. Think about how it's going to affect a business process and the results of that change. There are a ton of vendors to choose from, all with decent marketing and a promise that your life will get easier. But will it? You must do the research.

Technology isn't the disruptor to your firm, though it may sometimes feel like it, with constant updates and new inventions coming out daily. Being available in real time is the disruption. It's the fact that customers want to be connected to us all the time, through all available channels. Let's thank our mobile devices for that.

Tenet #2: Social Business (Not Social Media)

When I talk about social business, I'm not just talking about using social media via marketing, I mean really becoming a social business, and using your social channels to connect with your customers. Think about that for a minute.

I'm using social media tools to enhance my customers' experience. I'm not just blasting messages out in some one-sided way, which today, I think a lot of CPA firms are still doing. The messages are canned and impersonal, and many firm owners wonder why there is no ROI. This isn't just content marketing where you're giving them information and then leaving them be. This is a different animal. I allow my customers to connect with me on a personal-friend level. Just by the nature of doing that, that makes your business social.

At my firm, some of our customers reach out to us via Facebook and ask us tax questions. They ask us the types of questions that traditionally would have been asked via telephone or email. Instead my team and I get questions via Messenger. To our personal accounts! Imagine that. Not only are we friends with them via Facebook, but I, as the managing partner of the firm, must trust my employees to be able to field those messages properly. And I do. So, not only is it a whole new idea of friending your customer and being transparent with them but it's allowing your team to do the same thing.

Tenet #3: Value Pricing

Just say no to time and billing. Go ahead, you can do it. Those of you who have done it know the far-reaching impact of this great change. Think of it this way: Time and billing is focused on ourselves. It's a way of looking at only charging for inputs and not a result. Value pricing is focused on our customer. The customer doesn't care how long it takes, they just want their problem solved. If you want to be in a partnership or a relationship with someone, do you always want to talk about yourself? People don't want to be with others who always talk about themselves. But why is it when we engage with our customers in our firms (and our websites, for that matter) that we are always talking about ourselves? This is particularly true when we work from a model of time and billing.

Here's where alternative pricing comes in. It's time to experiment with fixed pricing and value pricing. Fixed pricing is when the service itself is priced, when the same level of transactions, same gross receipts, and same deliverables share the same price across all the customers. Value pricing is when the customer is priced, not the scope of the service. It's based on the customer's perceived value of the solution you are providing. It takes a lot more work in the proposal process and should only be done for engagements that exceed a specific amount. I combine the two pricing models in my firm. The key takeaway here is: Time and billing is focused on ourselves while value pricing is focused on our customer.

Tenet #4: Process

The last tenet to focus on when you are working to create a future-ready firm is your customer experience and process. And guess what, you can't improve a process if you can't identify the process. Too many firms really don't know what their processes are, or if they've evolved. Since they aren't typically giving them the attention they deserve, they aren't updated in a way that can increase efficiency and ease.

As a firm owner, you really need to identify and articulate your processes so that you can change them. Too many firms don't even know what their processes are because they've never been documented and therefore they've never been formally updated. This leads to inevitable chaos (and not the good kind) because team members are all doing firm processes differently

Being Radical is work.

Now, I know what you're thinking. When you start making all these changes, you start adding new technology, you start getting more social, you start updating your prices, suddenly now all your processes get disrupted and need to change.

And this is the reason why many CPAs prefer to stick their heads in the sand and not deal with reality. The disruption.

It's real. And if there's anything I've learned from the many CPAs who contacted me after my first book, it's that it's scary. I agree, and I know from my very own experience.

Therefore, we see old-school firms struggling. It's because they really need to rethink all their processes around these new developments. Cloud. Social. Pricing. Process. It's the fundamentals.

Think of it this way: A firm no longer has three days to get something done. If you're working in real time in QuickBooks Online, your customer sees that file exactly when you see it, and you don't have the option to have a team member work on it, a staff person review it, get a manager's input, and then turn it around two or three days later. It needs to be done in real-time, and that's what is creating the chaos in our firms. Customers' expectations have gone from hours to minutes! You better believe that if there's a live file and no one reviews it, that means we must get better at training team members upfront. Which again points to the importance of process and constantly staying on top of how work is flowing.

Files need to be done in real time, and that's what is creating the chaos in our firms

The future is bright.

As we move forward into the future, we must get better at setting the communication expectations correctly so that our customers don't feel the chaos that we feel internally. We've learned a lot over the last few years, and now we're older and wiser, with a lot more experience (and yes, confidence) under our belt. This book takes our beloved tenets to the next level and shares what my firm and my team have learned, as well as what the most progressive firms in the country are doing.

Many of you reading this are already Radical. This book will help you go deeper into your applications of our tenets offering tips, tricks, and strategies from those who have taken risks and changed the cultures of their firms. Consider it your roadmap to updating your new business model or revamping it all together. And if you're a managing partner of a midsized firm, kudos for picking up this book, I'm glad you're here!

Buckle up, you're in for a ride!

New Thinking From the Ground Up:
An Interview With Josh Zweig of LiveCA LLP

By Kayleigh Padar

Josh Zweig is the cofounder at LiveCA LLP, a chartered accounting firm of about 40 people that is run remotely, without a traditional office building. Three years ago, the entire business was just a sole proprietorship; now it is bringing in millions of dollars of revenue.

Their firm's biggest challenge is recruitment. "For smaller firms that don't have 20 college reps to go down to every school and recruit, it becomes increasingly hard to get word out that, there is an alternative here for people," Zweig said.

To combat this, leadership has focused on creating an exciting workplace culture that involves team building and bonding despite not seeing each other face-to-face every day.

"When we were talking about growing a firm, we said, 'what if we had nice people that were also accountants who knew how to talk to clients?'" Zweig says. "Now, looking back, we have these people. I think one of the things I'm most proud of is cultivating an environment where those kinds of people can thrive."

A major struggle for the firm is finding qualified people who fit well in the culture. To cultivate this environment, the team organizes different travel-based retreats throughout the year to encourage team bonding. For example, the team recently went "glamping" (glam camping), with a five-star chef and the opportunity to participate in lots of outdoor activities.

"You wake up in the morning, you have your coffee, you're looking at the mountains, and you're watching the team in their huddle, and everyone's so passionate about this thing. For me, that's a very proud moment of, 'look what we're building.'" Zweig said. "Our product is us, it's people. We're only as good as our people, only as good as our training, which, while we have processes, ultimately the wrong person is going to drive poor service," said Zweig.

College students transition easily into the firm, but it is hard to find the exact people who fit best in the firm culture, especially when most early graduates are considering joining large, well-known firms. The culture at LiveCA LLP also works well for accountants who would prefer to work occasionally remotely, as they travel.

One of Zweig's regrets is not planning, but rather waiting for things to go wrong before revising processes.

"If I look at where we made significant changes, it's because we screwed up and we went, 'Okay, we need to learn from this screw-up. What do we do?' It's not like we predicted many things. We're getting into that now."

He added: "If I could've done something different, it would've been correcting those processes before we expanded the team, which is always harder. What processes do we need to be that team of 80? Perhaps, had we [done] that, we would've been in a different position now."

As for building a firm, Zweig believes that an accounting firm is like any other small business.

"If you want to build a business, then there must be a brand, there must be unity, there must be a philosophy, there must be a vision, and there must be DNA for change, like any other business," Zweig said.

Their firm is an excellent example of envisioning new developments in the industry. The firm works in a virtual office space, experiments with different pricing strategies, and views the traditional tax return in a different light.

"The way we look at a tax return is, that it's the product of planning throughout the year. If you want someone that you have a long-term relationship with that will plan with you as your life changes, that's who we are. A big part of what we do and sell is that concept of a long-term relationship for a fixed price, with the deliverable being good tax planning throughout the year."

Different technology can produce tax returns, but the value for the customer is the human relationship that firms can build with clients. The value isn't in the tax return itself because the everyday person can do that independently. The idea of the New Firm is to sell the relationship that will eventually create the return.

New forms of pricing come along with the idea of selling a relationship. "The billable hour model doesn't offer much in the way of a deliverable, whereas what a fixed price package represents is some kind of product, like if you rent a car for a day," Zweig said.

While these changes can be hard to implement, all business owners must be ready to make them—no matter what industry or niche they are serving.

"What traditional firms, I think, are missing, is defining themselves," he said.

Kayleigh Padar is a college bound high school senior and an aspiring journalist. She is one of the Editor in Chiefs of her school newspaper, The Correspondent. *She has been working for New Vision CPA Group for three years.*

CHAPTER 1

The Radical Road to (Business) Transformation

When I wrote *The Radical CPA*, I thought that the four fundamental tenets would take us indefinitely into the future.

But I realize now the future demands more than that.

Yes, the four fundamental tenets are part of the New Firm model. However, I think there's a bigger overreaching process, aka management style, that needs to be defined.

It initially took me more than five years to develop and put into practice the ideas for the original Radical CPA book. The world was moving fast, but in the last two years it has been whizzing by. New technologies are coming out and being implemented like never before. Talent is demanding more. Processes and experiences need to be updated all the time. No longer is there an opportunity to wait till off-season to make a change.

Main Street America is also driving this change. Main Street businesses have a different expectation of what a CPA should be doing for them. This is driven by the consumer market, and also because Radical CPAs and vendors have pushed a new way of working and managing. As a result, our customers have new, more sophisticated and specific, expectations.

Defining Radical Today

I still believe we should use the term Radical. Being Radical means being very different from what is traditional or ordinary. It also means, as we know, having extreme political or social views that are not shared by most people—no matter if you're conservative or liberal.

The term Radical still applies because what we're doing to our firms and indirectly to the profession is fundamental to its core. It's abrupt, disruptive, unexpected, and far reaching. We are (and have been) shaking up the status quo. However, if you're new to this movement, you will learn that it's not just drama for the sake of drama. We are changing because our customers and the world around us are changing, and demanding we change with them.

The rallying cry that I proclaimed for CPAs in my first book is still true today:

Why should I be Radical?

A CPA must be Radicalized so they cannot be lulled into complacency.

It's as simple as that.

It's a proactive approach to managing a practice, instead of being driven by a reaction in their current firm.

You already know the story: The silent majority of employees are suspicious of management and don't feel heard. They see and experience the changes happening around them and they don't understand the resistance to change from practice leaders. You may even be feeling this yourself within your firm of one. This toxic condition within many firms is corrosive and detrimental. Employee frustrations are still mounting to the point of verbalization and indifference. And remember, an employee who is indifferent is by far more destructive to a firm than the outspoken team member who is leading a revolt. They can't wait any longer and neither could the initial core group of Radicals who started the movement years ago.

Today, however, I believe I have a stronger methodology to incorporate those four tenets and core principles. Innovation is not just a one-time business model change. I hate to say it, but the initial Radical changes we made to our firms will only take us so far. They were a solid beginning, but we have more a lot more work to do.

As other firms adopt the tenets into their own practices, I see many firms imitating others online. This is not a bad thing, as I believe this is what will keep these firm increasingly relevant moving forward, but I think it's a temporary solution. Innovation must be our best practices. We need to build it into our DNA.

How Market Demand Influences the Four Tenets

If you had asked me a few years ago how many firms were thinking about implementing value or fixed pricing, I would have said it was just a few.

Things are different today.

Firms are now learning about implementing new ways to price from big companies, such as Intuit, Xero, and Sage. Those companies realize that the market has changed and therefore have invested their marketing dollars to help transform a traditional accounting firm to one that is relevant to today's technology and customer-driven environment. Of course, these vendors sell software, and this marketing push is to increase adoption of their cloud products. This isn't a bad thing. With their marketing push comes education and more information for consumers to make smarter choices. As a result, small business owners now realize they have an alternative in how they work with a CPA. And that message is moving upstream as vendors such as Oracle, Microsoft, and Gartner are now pushing for the cloud and digital transformation with their customers as well. This is truly a good thing.

The middleman is now becoming minimalized or non-existent. Customers are going directly to the Internet or cloud and asking for the online products they want and need. These customers are not innovators; they are Joe Small Business and Sally Midsized Business. For as much as I thought the Internet was already mainstream, now more than ever, there are greater expectations for what it can accomplish. Our mobile workforce and lifestyle is driving this. People use apps every day in their lives, and they want the same option for business. Every business owner, whether it be a small or midsized business, has an expectation of using simple apps to run their business. They see everyday experiences based in design thinking during multiple events throughout their day.

Consumers experience positive and negative interactions in both the physical and the Internet world. Experiences are now being designed with a positive end in mind. Today's consumer has a different expectation of service and delight, and if they love what they experience, they will socially share.

Consumers compare their experiences, including the one with their CPA, to all the other experiences that they have had previously.

And let's be real: Our CPA experience is typically not up to par. This new world has created a hyper expectation that we all must meet. It requires us to truly develop business transformation as part of our core and find a completely new way to run a firm.

> And let's be real: Our CPA experience is typically not up to par.

The companies that have been able to deliver on that expectation are doing extremely well.

Technology venders are being pushed in new ways. Yet only some are meeting the challenge.

Karbon is Building a Practice Management Platform on Steroids: An Interview with Cofounder Ian Vacin

By Kayleigh Padar

Ian Vacin is the cofounder and vice president of product marketing at Karbon, a software designed to help firms improve their processes. He described why process improvement is vital to a functioning firm.

"You can't keep operating at the same pace using the existing processes that you have today," Vacin said. "Your clients want more value day after day, and you need to provide it to them. When on the road, most firms that I see are traditional and don't even have their processes defined. They aren't innovative, they aren't growing and don't have a starting point to do so."

Processes are often individualized for different clients, and Karbon is designed to help managers create and delegate checklists and tasks to the employees best suited for each job. While over a majority of the process remains the same throughout the firm, other parts need to be flexible to ensure each client is best served by the right person in the practice.

"For firms today, data is in multiple places and not at their fingertips. Combine this with the pain and effort of documenting everything, and you find people putting data wherever they can. The result is that no one is able to find what they need, when they need it," Vacin said.

Basically, Karbon unites a team with a singular place to work together. The software allows for users to manage their files collectively, collaborate on the work, and assign emails to each other, making it possible for everyone in the firm to have visibility across the work and the full relationship with a given client.

"The problem is that communications sit inside of the silos of each person's machine, typically in their inbox. When someone calls and you pick up the phone, you don't necessarily know what has happened beforehand. This problem only gets exacerbated by the number of employees in the firm and the number of systems in place," Vacin said.

Some firms may feel as though there's a lack of communication within the team. Karbon connects members' technology so that time is saved and unnecessary computer searching is eliminated.

"It's that peace of mind knowing I can go somewhere, and understand what's going on across all the different people in the firm and across all my clients," Vacin said.

This software doesn't alter firms' processes or take care of any work, but instead enables employees to finish work in a more efficient way while ensuring that each team member is equipped with the maximum amount of information available.

"Karbon isn't the place you actually do work. Karbon is that place for you to manage and oversee it to ensure that the work is getting done. It lets you know what to do next and springboards you to the right place to complete the work. Karbon provides you peace of mind, knowing that every moment of the day, you have all the information at your fingertips," he said.

Most firms using this technology are either younger or have aggressive plans to grow. They seem to be finding that this is the most efficient way to keep track of everything that is going on in the digital realm of the office.

"They have determined that their best way to the highest profitability is ultimately being able to be the most efficient that they can," Vacin said. "They are going to leverage technology as an advantage for themselves and a way to distance themselves from the competition."

What exactly is business transformation?

In Scott Anthony's February 2016 Harvard Business Review article, "What Do You Really Mean by Business Transformation," he talks about three different categories of effort: operational (what you are currently doing better, faster, or cheaper), core transformation (what you are doing in a fundamentally different way), and strategic (how you are changing the essence of a company).

What I think is genius about Anthony's differentiation of these three models is that they relate perfectly to how we run our accounting firms. Many CPAs are stuck in the operational model, or, to put it another way, have just added in technology (like adopting the cloud) but really haven't changed any of their processes. They are just adding expensive technology onto a broken firm model. It's the Band-Aid approach.

Core transformation is where The Radical CPA model lives. Anthony points to Netflix as an example of this, as the company has moved away from sending DVDs through the mail to streaming video content via the Web. It's also transitioned from just distributing other entertaining content to creating its own. Netflix is a remarkable example of how tuning into customer preferences informs new offerings and how it stays ahead of the curve. Wouldn't you say the Radical CPAs have done this with accounting firms? I would.

The strategic model is our challenge. It's the structure on how we build the New Firm 2.0. This is beyond what we already know. And as Anthony wrote, "Executed successfully, strategic transformation reinvigorates a company's growth engine. Poor execution leads naysayers to pounce and complain that a company should have 'stuck to its knitting.'"

The Next Step for Radicals

For Radical CPAs, this is the next step in our business model innovation:

Innovation at such a high level that our fathers (and mothers) won't even recognize our companies as CPA firms.

This will become more apparent as artificial intelligence (AI) takes over and accounting is truly machine-driven. A CPA will use data completely differently than he or she does today; we don't know what we don't know yet. The foundational structure of our firms need to Radically change to allow for this new automation and innovation.

What we find in the New Firms is that technology is taking over the grunt work, and, in many cases, the actual output or what we used to sell. We are advising on technology but embracing the automation and the removal of old data collection/entry jobs as well as the final deliverable. We are exploring and redefining what the CPA should do with the old report and typically the what-we-are-selling part looks nothing like it did.

The easiest example is the compilation, which has now become a real-time financial statement. The next level is then the forecast that lives online as well, with the "what-if's" being done in real-time with the customer watching. There is no two-week lag time between a what-if and a conversation. Using a forecasting tool such as Futrli brings vast new depth to real-time advisory. So, we are ready for it and aware of it as it happens and are nimble enough to capitalize on it. We need to Radicalize practice management with accounting, tax, and audit as the main ingredients and serve them with a side of data. Data is the catalyst for all change. The hardest part of data is making sure it's the right data and that it's complete. What is the right data? Where do we find it? How do we categorize it? It's the data that makes up a financial statement, but it's not the traditional ratios we create from them, as managerial accounting will need to be included. Accountants also must remember that not all data is objective, and sometime the best data includes subjectivity. We must remind ourselves that our future sales will not be anything like they are today. They have already moved from an hour to a result. We must step up and learn how to shift our firms to produce new products that are market-driven and future-ready. The tools in this book will help you do just that.

The good news is, we're now on an upswing. We have greater CPA adoption of technology and more choices in the way we run our firms. And, we are getting better tools from vendors. According to CPA.com we are in the early majority of cloud adoption, but the numbers don't lie: Fewer than 10 percent of all firms are 100 percent cloud driven.

A Wolters Kluwer whitepaper, "Game Plan for the Future," addresses how firms can expand their offerings and branch out to include more high-value services for their clients. According to the survey in the white paper, firms that use end-to-end integrated solutions can offer broader services, especially collaborative and consulting services, as well as other offerings. Firms with integrated solutions performed higher than firms with unintegrated solutions. The easiest way to integrate is to have all your data live in the cloud. Lots of firms are catching on to this; however, often it's only some customers or one department within the firm that are on board.

When data lives in the cloud, a whole new world of artificial intelligence will open up, but more on that later in the book. The entire firm must change to reach the full return on investment.

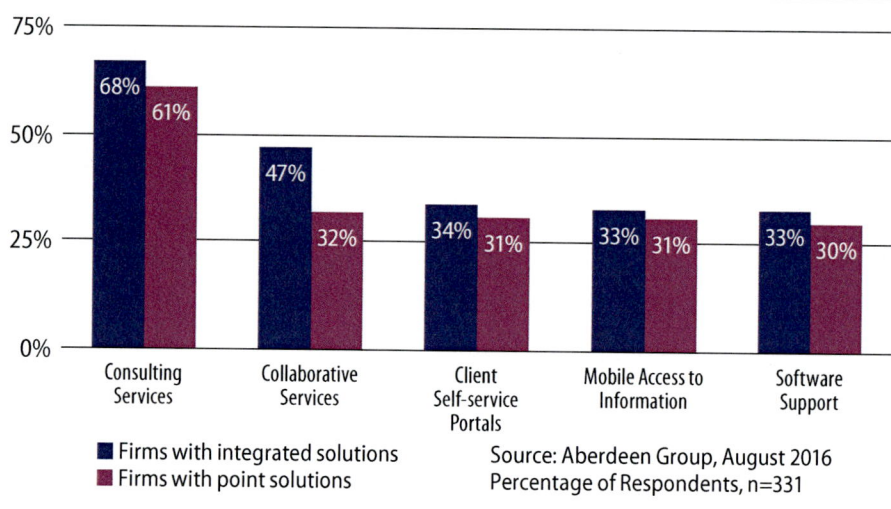

Firms with integrated solutions
Firms with point solutions
Source: Aberdeen Group, August 2016
Percentage of Respondents, n=331

Technology improves the breadth of services.
Source: Wolters Kluwer whitepaper "Game Plan for the Future: Are You and Your Clients in Sync?"

Not surprisingly, we have startups to thank for this movement. Bench.io and inDinero are pushing the boundaries in this space. These startups are selling outsourced accounting to small businesses. They use Facebook advertising and other digital marketing tools to sell services. They have venture capital behind them. It's been interesting to see how VC money has determined the opportunities in this space, while Top 100 firms have not yet figured out how to address their own market.

Client accounting services or outsourced bookkeeping are staples of many firms. Yet because of their fear of change, many firms haven't been able to fully experience the benefits of newer technology and automation. If a firm is stuck in billing by the hour, there is no incentive to change or improve a process. The firm gets caught in the price of the technology and misses the savings in the cost of labor. The firm doesn't realize that one team member can do exponentially more work with the new technology. In the billable hour model, improving the process with technology reduces your sale price. Therefore, there is no incentive to innovate. These firms are like the Netflix model. If they don't switch to video streaming soon and get rid of the DVD model, they will go the way of Blockbuster. They can cannibalize their own market. If they don't move soon, someone else will. The opportunities to scale are becoming within reach, and firms are finally understanding what cloud capacity can accomplish.

One firm that has demonstrated that they understand the concept of business transformation is BDO. In 2016, they announced a partnership with Intuit to launch BDO*Drive*, an integrated cloud-based financial management and accounting service.

> *In the billable hour model, improving the process with technology reduces your sale price. Therefore, there is no incentive to innovate. These firms are like the Netflix model. If they don't switch to video streaming soon and get rid of the DVD model, they will go the way of Blockbuster.*

At first it struck me as strange; it seemed so out of their marketplace. However, they had a strategic reason up their sleeves.

"BDODrive fundamentally improves upon the traditional concept of business outsourcing. It gives clients the power of rich information, business intelligence, and insight that enables them to operate more efficiently and effectively," said Kelly Johnson, partner and national practice leader for business services and outsourcing at BDO USA.

Some of the key features delivered through the BDO*Drive* service offering are accounting and financial management, online payments, auto bank feeds and reconciliation, business data analytics, secure document management, and customized reporting of key performance indicators delivered in real-time with 24/7 mobile access. KPIs are data snapshots in pictures. This is the first step to redefining how we deliver financial data.

CHAPTER 2
Dear Midsized Firms (Yes, You Can Change)

In a traditional firm, the partner is the center of everything—from technical knowledge to relationship management to operations. Everything stems from the partner, and, depending on the size of the firm, there may not even be one true managing partner. However, under this model, what happens when something happens to that partner?

It's not a pretty sight.

Sure, team members and other partners step in and pick up the pieces, but the firm may not be viable for an extended period. I would argue (and often do) that if technology is at the core of your practice, your firm has a much better opportunity for success if you should find yourself in this circumstance.

I've always believed this to be true, but this past tax season, my firm worked when I needed it to.

The last week in March, I ended up having urgent surgery. I was told before surgery I would be out for four to six weeks. I was never worried about my firm or cash flow because we have the people, technology, and systems in place for my firm to run, well, on autopilot.

Could you say that about your firm? Would you consider your firm a viable business?

My firm runs with upfront package pricing so hours and bills didn't need my review for us to get paid. We use CCH Axcess so I could see every tax return moving through my office, right from my bed. I set up my firm so I do very little billable work, and, as a result, my team didn't miss a beat with customer interactions and getting the work done. Having all those elements in place allowed my firm to run independently of its owner for a while so I could recover.

Does the above freak you out?

Are you ready to get started on a transformational journey to running a firm completely differently than the firm in which you grew up? Are you ready to hear from other firm owners about the successes they have had in their transformation?

Are you ready to put in your time and money to invest today in your current firm? Can you give up some of your cash dividends and reinvest them as part of your fiduciary duty to the firm you started or joined years ago? The current tax law suggests that most likely, much of your current income is going to taxes. Is your retirement and your family's legacy worth the reinvestment?

Would you like to create a utopian firm that will live into the future?

Why utopian?

To make sure we're all working from the same definition, let's look at how Merriam-Webster defines the term:

> ### Definition of *utopian* from Merriam-Webster
>
> 1. of, relating to, or having the characteristics of a utopia; *especially*: having impossibly ideal conditions especially of social organization
> 2. proposing or advocating impractically ideal social and political schemes: *utopian idealists*
> 3. impossibly ideal: visionary *recognized the utopian nature of his hopes* —C. S. Kilby
> 4. believing in, advocating, or having the characteristics of utopian socialism: *utopian doctrines, utopian novels*

A utopian firm beats any "firm of the future" because it includes a feeling of contentment and happiness. This is something I believe most, if not all, firms of the past—and even today—lack or lost somewhere along the way.

An ideal firm's conditions are created by growth, technology, innovation, and happiness. Talent stays for the long term, less hours are worked, and firms are still profitable. Utopian is unique to each culture. See why I like the term?

Unfortunately, we probably won't see unicorns or rainbows along the way, but we will see a new attitude of innovation and engagement taking over. Let's get started. Transformation is on its way.

Our pain points are opportunities.

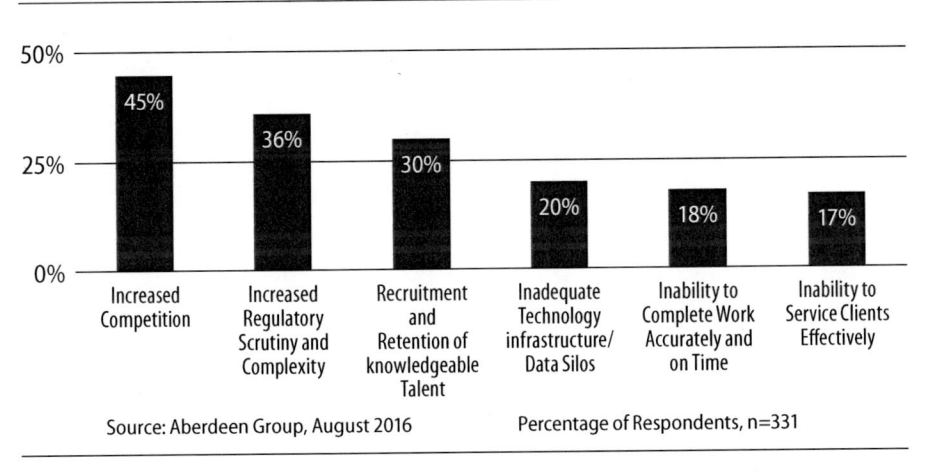

Challenge	Percentage
Increased Competition	45%
Increased Regulatory Scrutiny and Complexity	36%
Recruitment and Retention of knowledgeable Talent	30%
Inadequate Technology infrastructure/ Data Silos	20%
Inability to Complete Work Accurately and on Time	18%
Inability to Service Clients Effectively	17%

Source: Aberdeen Group, August 2016. Percentage of Respondents, n=331

Top challenges for tax and accounting firms. Source: Wolters Kluwer whitepaper "Game Plan for the Future: Are You and Your Clients in Sync?"

Opportunities are everywhere. As a successful business owner, you already know this. But when you look at your firm's biggest challenges, do you see opportunities? Opportunities are always openings for innovation or change. As a firm owner, you have a choice: You can address your challenges about the changing market head on or you can just hide your head in the sand and leave it for the next generation to tackle.

My question to you is this: Why aren't firms adapting to the issues of today? Why does it feel like everything is so doom and gloom? Has the profession always felt this way? I don't remember the despair and fear that seems to have taken over the profession. It feels like a bunch of grumpy old men, no pun intended. But I think the solution is attainable, with just a little strategy and effort.

Innovation needs to happen every day. My firm is moving into the wealth management space where I plan to Radicalize how personal financial planning is done. Maybe your firm wants to add another specialty or change up the way audits are delivered. Like I said earlier, innovation must be part of your DNA, and you need to keep reinventing your firm and your offerings. It's all about incremental innovation, friends. Say it with me: Every day innovation!

OK, but really, what is innovation? We all know it's a heavily overused buzzword. Still, I like to say it because it perfectly captures what is happening to our profession. According to Merriam-Webster again, innovation can be defined simply as a "new idea, method, or device." However, innovation is often also viewed as the application of better solutions that meet new requirements, unarticulated needs, or existing market needs. This is accomplished through more effective products, processes, services, technologies, or business models that are readily available to markets, governments, and society.

Innovation is inspired by speed and experimentation. Let's be real: Many CPA firms rely on safe, tried, and tested processes. The system is built to protect the status quo and reject anything that may disrupt those secure processes. So, innovation in most CPA firms is an oxymoron.

Another reason why some CPA firms tend to reject innovation is because it often reduces billable hours. And we all know how much CPAs tend to love their billable hours. Innovation causes you to do things more quickly and cheaply, which is less expensive for the customer and in turn makes less money for you if you bill by the hour.

That's why pricing is a key factor in innovation.

Innovation can potentially cannibalize your existing business. However, it is far better for that to happen by you, than by another firm. I see this happening every day as the midsized firms lose customers to small firms who utilize technology better and are creating digital transformations for these new customers. Those legacy relationships with the firm suddenly (and, yes, painfully) become immaterial, as the innovation is more important.

But this is the case for most CPA firms. There are some firms that are knocking it out of the park.

If You're Not Disrupting, You're Not Doing it Right: An Interview with Dean Quiambao of Armanino LLP

By Kayleigh Padar

Dean Quiambao, a CPA and business development partner at Armanino LLP, a Top 25 firm, works hard to incubate revolutionary ideas within his firm to help it grow and modernize as the world around him changes.

"Do your activity, because activity breeds activity," said Quiambao. "And I say this all the time, you keep hitting singles and the next thing you know you're going to pop a triple out of nowhere. You're going to make your own luck, you're going to make something happen because you're constantly doing something."

Located in a hub of innovation, Silicon Valley, Armanino LLP has always had change in its DNA. "Here, disruption is normal. It's expected. If you're not disrupting, you're not doing it right," Quiambao said.

Quiambao believes the biggest reason for their modernization and success is that their team won't shy away from an attempt. "We are willing to try things. We fail a lot of times. We've done things that haven't worked out, but we're willing to try. And we have lots of people that are walking, living, breathing examples of innovation around the office," Quiambao said.

Another large factor that helps the team to modernize is the firm's mission statement. "We put up our mission statement, and our mission statement is what we all hold true to our heart. We want to be the most entrepreneurial, innovative CPA consulting firm in the country that has a positive impact on the lives of our client," Quiambao said.

Although the mission statement is simple, it provides a very big goal to accomplish and something to constantly strive for within the firm. "From the top down, innovation is just kind of what we do. And we talk about it all the time," Quiambao said.

Quiambao knows it's in their secret sauce, but here is how they get tactical for inorganic growth. "Once you do a couple big inorganic deals, mergers, you bring on 75 people or 100 people. You say 'Okay, there are some bumps.'" After merging in two larger firms, and knowing they would be continuing to do more mergers, now they have an integration team.

"It's our SWAT team of people that include IT, finance, all of the HR, Armanino University, our onboarding program, all of the administrative people, all of what we call operations. Our operations SWAT team goes in together and looks at a merger.

Then we assess and create a plan on how this is all going to work," Quiambao said.

"To me that is real life. So now, by the time you get to someone like TravisWolff in Dallas, everyone feels comfortable. This is what we do, we grow organically and inorganically. The second that I feel comfortable in my job, 'Okay good, we're doing this, we're doing that,' something changes. We buy a line of business. Like dude, just when I got comfortable." Quiambao added: "That's word to the wise. Right? That's how it's going to be here at Armanino. That's just what we do."

Activating Innovation

Ideas are a dime a dozen, but very few accountants have the insight or time to carry out the steps of translating their idea into a workable solution. CPAs are exposed daily to opportunities to innovate, yet because our firm cultures don't necessarily celebrate or even acknowledge them, they get lost. Ideas can come in many forms for many things—but many of us want our ideas to translate into revenue. Later, I will share with you a systemized way to transfer ideas into New Firm products that can be sold.

Many of us have no idea what to do with our ideas. My first hire, Alex, who is now a principal in my firm, would ask me to come into her office in the morning and have me shake my ideas (so to speak) out on her desk. We used to just write them down on a yellow legal pad. She is the executer in our firm, a COO of sorts. I needed that. I was getting carried away with ideas, and she helped me bring them to earth. We would write them down, some never to be seen again. I've always had more ideas than time. However, via trial and error, we figured out a way to capture those ideas to build on them. Our whole team was involved. That is what today's firm must do. Is that happening in midsized firms? Who has the time? Everybody is either trying to bill hours or trying to prove their value to the partnership group. Or they are in meetings.

We cannot just innovate on process. It's not enough. We need to innovate around what it is we sell, how we create products, and how we market those products. We need more than a new business model. We need a new set of ingredients that we bake into the culture of our firm. Organic is better.

Translating our ideas into workable solutions requires a desire to embrace entrepreneurship. It means the firm is open and willing to listen to new ideas. So, they are shared openly and embraced, or at least acknowledged and prioritized. The team has the transparency and a solid understanding of the why. They have a crystallized vision of the environmental business landscape as well as access to a roadmap that covers team and client expectations, their individual role, and the strategy that illustrates the holistic goals of the firm.

I know what you're thinking: But my firm is entrepreneurial! We live and breathe entrepreneurial!

Really? I tend to disagree.

Innovation takes time and space to think. It's hard to think when firms are focused on production-based hours. These hours billed produce firm revenue from efficiency that was born in the industrial revolution era. Where factory-like ideals and production hours were celebrated. Firms act like factories today, producing billable hour after billable hour. Teams are managed like factory workers and give little time to "get out of the production line" to work on something else. And employees are measured on production. Think realization rates. Innovation gets halted dead in its tracks.

Our cultures eat the opportunity to innovate.

Thinking like an entrepreneur is not always easy for us. In fact, sometimes it feels very uncomfortable. To put it gently, CPAs by nature are somewhat risk averse. However, I believe that with our deep knowledge of the market, our unique set of technical skills, and a little entrepreneurial training, we can be masters of this domain. I've seen incredibly smart CPAs do phenomenal work brainstorming at roundtables. The problem is when they "go home" to their firms, the innovation switch turns off. Why? Because their cultures eat innovation via billable hours and regulatory compliance seasons.

> I've seen incredibly smart CPAs do phenomenal work brainstorming at roundtables. The problem is when they "go home" to their firms, the innovation switch turns off. Why? Because their cultures eat innovation via billable hours and regulatory compliance seasons.

If there's one thing you walk away with in reading this book, let it be this: CPAs, it's up to you to lead in your firms. It's up to you to illustrate what innovation means in the context of practice management. The economy is increasingly motivated by innovation that is led by business. As a business owner's most trusted advisor, we do a shockingly poor job at creating ongoing consistent opportunities for innovations in our firms. How are we modeling our cutting-edge knowledge and insight? Many CPAs aren't, and instead are getting blown away by the competition. And sorry, just adopting cloud technologies isn't innovating. It's reaching for low-hanging fruit.

How valuable is a new idea?

> In this fast-moving and hyper-competitive environment, delaying decisions around the shift change is the same as not investing.

This is the question every CPA is asking right now. What's the ROI? Or as futurist Tom Hood of the Maryland Association of CPAs would say, "What's the return of not investing?" Consider the cost/risk of not investing, of being left behind. In this fast-moving and hyper-competitive environment, delaying decisions around the shift change is the same as not investing.

Never, as CPAs, have we been given the opportunities or a blueprint to solve this challenge. But now we have more tools and resources at our fingertips, and our peers are starting to move in this direction as well. Consider these questions as you start innovating:

- What is the difference between a good idea and an opportunity?
- How does one evaluate its potential?
- How does one deliver a product to the market?
- What are the challenges within the financial marketplace to launch a new idea?
- How can a CPA capture and generate this value through the process and obtain compensation for the effort?

Sourcing Ideas

Ideas and inspiration go hand in hand and can be found anywhere. From the ugly and mundane to the most beautiful and stunning. Many entrepreneurs come up with ideas for a business because they couldn't find what they wanted. Something was missing. There was a gap. Frustration was present. Problems are excellent sources of new ideas. When you are angry about something, that is the perfect place to start. Most people will try to make it better. Hence, why I left my old firm.

Market opportunities that reduce cost are also a source of new ideas. Think about it—those who have tight resources need to be creative to meet goals. Ideas also come in the form of customer demands creating products and services for a new niche that was nonexistent up until that point.

The search for new ideas is an attitude more than a task. It does not include intentionally looking for new ideas as much as maintaining an attitude of continued skepticism to improve our environment. A culture that's open to new ideas has space and capacity to think; it allows for research and development (R&D). Our New Vision culture allows for failure, but more importantly, we encourage the openness needed to try something new. Employees need to be encouraged and given opportunities for experimentation. Time and resources must be allocated to this activity. This is really a mindset that rewards new ideas and improving the status quo.

It's about accepting suggestions for improvements. It's about taking your team out to learn new things, not making them attend all CPE via webinar. It's about embracing an idea that fails, saying, "OK, let's stop this and try again." It's about stopping an implementation that's getting sideswiped with customer work and saying, "Let's pause this project and pick it up again." It's not: "This didn't work, it's all over." It's about attitude to embrace uncertainty sometimes but to know that somehow, we all get out alive. It's about a leader who allows for mistakes to happen. People say our firm acts like a startup, yet we just celebrated our 11th anniversary.

This is why the billable hour is so detrimental to CPA firms.

Introducing the Fifth Tenet: The Business Model

Many Radicals have already made the shift to pricing by value or a fixed price agreement. Yet, they are still tracking time. When we value our team on an hour, it leaves almost no time for innovation to occur. An incremental shift could be to allow for a certain number of innovation hours per week. However, once again, this is a huge limit on creating an innovative culture.

Depending on who you ask, there are a bazillion ways or categories of innovation. In my first book, I had a very linear way of looking at the outside influences that were happening to my firm, and I outlined them in the four tenets. Now I believe innovation can happen in every inch of our practice.

It's gone beyond technology or the cloud, communication or social, pricing, process, or experience. Innovation has found its way into our overall business model. Remember Anthony's third model of effort: strategy (changing the essence of a company). Its power is going to come from new cultures that create products instead of selling time because they will have continuous innovation and ideas built into their DNA. We must move from a culture of delivery to a culture of learning. Firms will have a financial data focus, but what we will end up selling will not look like what we sell today.

Today I believe the four tenets and the fifth tenet (the business model) aren't a beginning or an end to innovation. They are principles that need to be applied to specific products within a CPA firm, and consistently improved. Those specific products are ones we are more familiar with, and those that we are not, such as Blockchain or Internet of Things (IoT).

Is the profession ready for the future?

Yesterday	Today and the Future
As a profession, we should be past… • The cloud • Social • Mobile • Website & digital content	Let's help the profession embrace… • IoT • Big data • AI / Cognitive computing • Augmented reality • Voice interfaces • Blockchain • Machine learning • Advisory services offerings

Innovation based on customer product. Source: cpa.com

Before we can really dive into the fifth tenet, let's explore innovation. Everybody wants it, but not everybody has it. There are many formulas to create it, but how many are successful?

What are the barriers to innovation?

I don't have to tell you that you can suck the life out of anything innovative more quickly than you allow it to spring to life. In accounting firms, innovation isn't usually in our nature. Barriers to innovation and inspiration are everywhere and can creep up on you, even when you think your firm is "innovative." Here's a starting list of how these barriers play out in a typical firm:

- **Organizational.** This includes upholding the status quo no matter what, a lack of strong infrastructure, a lack of insight and comparative data as to what other competitors are doing, and blind succession, meaning just following in a former leader's footsteps, well, just because.
- **Regulatory.** It probably won't surprise you that ongoing regulation updates are a huge obstacle to innovation. With most of our time being spent deciphering what's new and what new updates to bring our customers, innovation takes a back seat. Outside demands and a compressed, stressful tax season also play a role in decreasing a firm's innovation.
- **Market.** If you follow the market, you won't get anywhere. We need to be leaders in our industry and with our clients. If you look to see what your top three competitors are doing, and they are all staying safe in their old-school ways, then believe me, any innovation that may be possible is dying. The market isn't moving fast enough, but that doesn't mean you can't be moving the needle yourself.
- **Financial.** I know why many firms don't see innovation—they are still billing by the hour! It's profitable, I realize. But it's not sustainable. I wrote about this profusely in my first book and I will say it again: Billing by the hour is a short-term solution to a major practice management growth issue. You will not grow as fast or as competitive as you want to be when you are still billing for every 15 minutes of your time.
- **Technological.** Vendors have been doing an OK job keeping up with our needs. They could be doing better. Clunky technology and frustrated employees can be obstacles to innovation. But tech can also inspire people to make things better. The cloud is still slow to catch on among CPAs, and that keeps our tools in the middle of the road.
- **Cultural.** CPAs often promote themselves as something they're not. Have you looked at the website of any accounting firm lately? The word "innovative" is everywhere. But are they truly? I seriously doubt it.

CPAs look at the past very well. But when we talk future, it's a different story. We know the typical personality features of a CPA—risk adverse, detailed, and perfectionist to a fault. Innovation calls for mistakes. When you innovate, and put yourself out there and start something new or do something differently, you will make mistakes. It comes with the territory. You must be able to pick yourself up, dust yourself off, and start over. Review points don't grow innovators. With very little upfront training and lots of negative reinforcement, firms stifle innovation or even a little out-of-the-box risk taking.

But enough about the barriers to innovation. I'm sure you are very familiar with those struggles. For both new and more established firms, there is no reason your firm can't produce the opportunity to innovate every day. Our Radical movement started with small firms. We were nicknamed "the agile firms." Why? Because we could move as the market moved. However, things have changed, and bigger firms are getting nimbler. I don't believe you have to be small to be innovative in your firm anymore. It's a mindset and a desire to be Radical. We have some powerful large Radical firms among us, proving that you don't have to be small to be innovative.

A Midsized Firm That Transitioned to Radical Successfully: An Interview With Carl Famiglietti

"The position makes the person," said Carl Famiglietti, managing partner of Moody, Famiglietti & Andronico, a 160-person firm located in Tewksbury, MA. His firm has undergone Radical changes since he took the helm in 2004, a time that he calls "The Reset." Carl has learned a lot as he has focused on building an organization for perpetuity.

It began with his acceptance of fiduciary duty to the firm. Famiglietti saw the need for firm leadership to put down their wallets and focus on the future by putting a dollar investment into the firm. It's paid off immensely.

He believes that if a partnership team isn't willing to change, then it might be time for a new team. For him, a business model must begin with a partner compensation plan and a new partnership agreement. Luckily, they were all on board, and are moving with grace toward a utopian firm.

Famiglietti said that everyone in his firm has an equal voice and an equal opportunity to make a valuable contribution. At MFA, there are no titles, and every team member can be a leader. It is an egalitarian model.

Since the changes, he's found that his organization is more collaborative, open, filled with self-discovery and a learning enterprise since before The Reset. He said the profession "self-selects" highly ethical people, and if given the freedom, a great culture can metastasize and grow. His team exercises good judgement and the firm has a less than five percent turnover rate. As a result, they have no worries recruiting talent. They are growing organically and he will tell you the proof is in his bottom line. He is happy with their healthy P&L.

MFA is a value pricing firm and doesn't keep time. Everything is priced up front and Famiglietti says this is key. From his point of view, many firms understate and don't price for their value. He said timesheets and utilization rates are demeaning to customers, team members, and everyone involved. They squash innovation and don't work when selling intellectual capital. There is little harmony in a firm with timesheets because they cannibalize.

MFA has undergone significant changes since The Reset; Famiglietti says that changing stimulates more changes and that change management "isn't a worry because their firm is now organically changing all the time. "Unleashed leadership and alignment with the firm's "why" attracts a line of customers who are open and forward-thinking and want professionals who help with their businesses. It's because of this MFA customers "come for impact," and know that they will get it.

You gotta be agile.

Let's talk about what "agile" means and why you need to embrace this way of being. Being a self-proclaimed techie, I'm kind of psyched that agile comes from a software definition.

Agile software development describes a set of principles under which requirements and solutions evolve through the collaborative effort of self-organizing, cross-functional teams. It advocates adaptive planning, evolutionary development, early delivery, and continuous improvement, and it encourages rapid and flexible response to change. These principles support the definition and continuing evolution of many software development methods.

The term agile was first coined for this in 2001, in the *Manifesto for Agile*

Software Development, and although originally written as *Agile* (with a capital A) this is progressively becoming deprecated.

Although I believe Radical firms don't follow an Agile model in its truest form, agile teams within CPA firms do exist, and move faster than possible even though they are faced with constricting external regulations. Also, to state the obvious, the inherent nature of our work is not creating software. However we do create products. But what New Firm teams have figured out is to use Agile principles to consistently innovate and continuously improve their firms.

Take a look at the website of the Agile Alliance (agilealliance.org). There you will find a ton of resources about agility as it relates to technology. Their mission? To support people who explore and apply Agile values, principles, and practices to make building software solutions more effective, humane, and sustainable.

Agile values:
- **Individuals and interactions** over processes and tools
- **Working software** over comprehensive documentation
- **Customer collaboration** over contract negotiation
- **Responding to change** over following a plan

Here are the Agile Alliance's 12 Principles, which are based on the Agile Manifesto.

1. Our highest priority is to satisfy the customer through early and continuous delivery of valuable software.
2. Welcome changing requirements, even late in development. Agile processes harness change for the customer's competitive advantage.
3. Deliver working software frequently, from a couple of weeks to a couple of months, with a preference to the shorter timescale.
4. Business people and developers must work together daily throughout the project.
5. Build projects around motivated individuals. Give them the environment and support they need, and trust them to get the job done.
6. The most efficient and effective method of conveying information to and within a development team is face-to-face conversation.
7. Working software is the primary measure of progress.

8. Agile processes promote sustainable development. The sponsors, developers, and users should be able to maintain a constant pace indefinitely.
9. Continuous attention to technical excellence and good design enhances agility.
10. Simplicity—the art of maximizing the amount of work not done—is essential.
11. The best architectures, requirements, and designs emerge from self-organizing teams.
12. At regular intervals, the team reflects on how to become more effective, then tunes and adjusts its behavior accordingly.

We think of an agile process in terms of releasing a good product while continually improving on it. Of course it is a good product, it inherently follows all regulatory rules and standards. We still uphold our ethics and all the other values of a being a CPA. The only thing that really changes is how fast our ability is to reiterate new ideas. It's okay to adopt Agile principals a little bit at time.

If we take this mindset we can continuously improve. If we continuously improve, we will always be relevant and we'll always have new opportunities for innovation.

Ask the Agility Expert: A Q&A With Donny C. Shimamoto, CPA, CITP, CGMA and Managing Director of IntrapriseTechKnowlogies LLC

JP: **Can you describe what your firm does?**

DS: We help transform CPA firms in a couple of ways. One is to help them embrace the cloud in a reasonable manner. The second is to embrace new approaches of working. You could even maybe say that we help them become Radical firms.

JP: **Who is your customer?**

DS: A typical customer for us will be any small to midsized organization that's going through a lot of change and transformation. What we often bring in is the innovation piece, which is the technology piece, but we do it from a CPA perspective. Meaning that a lot of our focus is on enterprise risk management—enterprise meaning holistic, not big. It's about policy and controls and the balancing of risk with reward and looking at the concept of bringing internal controls around a change that's occurring. Not just from a financial standpoint but also from a technology standpoint. Then also from a people standpoint.

JP: **How would you apply Agile principles to the work that you do?**

DS: Transformation is a long process. It's normally a two- to three-year process. Agile helps us balance the long-term vision of where the organization wants to go while showing incremental improvements and changes all along the way. Through Agile, we're able to demonstrate the benefit of the changes back to the client, as well as validate that the long-term vision is where they actually want to go. Sometimes we'll see as we start to work with them and they realize the implications of certain types of changes that they're asking to have occur, they may decide, "Well, maybe that might not be for us, or maybe that needs to be a little later and not now." It allows us to more quickly adjust and assure that there's value delivered all along the transformation that we're leading them through.

Probably the biggest advantage that we get from Agile is the fact that even within an engagement, that we can adjust and ensure that we're achieving the client's objectives, and that we can also still provide the value that we think we should provide within that engagement while staying within budget. That's where, if you're working with a set checklist and a non-mutable way that you're always doing the same thing over and over and over, that's not going to allow you to adjust as the client's needs change.

JP: **I know you have an IT background. Have you studied Agile or have you just seen it as far as business application?**

DS: I've seen it, and done it, and reviewed it, and audited it, and whatever else.

JPS: **How does each principle below apply to a firm engagement?**

Principle: *Our highest priority is to satisfy the customer through early and continuous delivery of valuable software.*

DS: The concept behind that is really looking at what they would conceptualize as incremental delivery of product. Rather than defining the entire thing up front, it's about really looking at how do we do it piece by piece as we go along. If you look at the audit from a fundamental standpoint, that is the audit. We do the risk assessment, we start to do some testing around controls. We then, based upon the results that we see from testing of controls, you go in and you do substantive. Based upon whether it passes or doesn't pass, you go do additional substantive. Then you pull everything back together again. The audit process in and of itself is designed very nicely to follow that principle.

JP: **To me it's kind of working in collaboration with a client to create the deliverable as opposed to doing it all and then saying, here it is.**

DS: You are correct. It's about validating along the way rather than it being this black hole of, "Okay, give us all your information," and we disappear for several months and then, "Oh, here's the output. That wasn't what you were expecting? Well, let's go back and revisit the whole thing."

Principle: *Build projects around motivated individuals, give them an environment and support they need and trust them to get the job done.*

JP: **How do CPA firms currently not achieve the above principle and what is something that maybe they could do to help them meet those goals?**

DS: That's where your whole message around the old-school versus new comes in… The new concept would be that you're basically empowering their staff to service the customer or client, versus the old-school version would be, well, the partner is the primary client conduit and everything flows through there. Also from an old versus new perspective, just follow the checklist and do what the checklist says, compared to, let's figure out whether the checklist actually makes sense and what things do we need to adjust in the checklist as we go along.

Principle: *Continuous attention to technical excellence and good design enhances agility.*

DS: It's about making sure that you're balancing the overall architecture and construct of what you're building versus being locked into individual steps. It's, keep in mind the end and it's about not taking shortcuts, and about making sure that even though we're building this piece by piece, that each piece has a strong sense of quality around it. That's what that principle says.

Stop talking, start doing

Recently, I went to an event on innovation, and I met one of the inventors of Google Glass, Tom Chi. At that same conference, I went to a session on rapid prototyping and realized that's what we were doing in my firm—organically. Rapid prototyping changes how people approach problems. Fast and cheap prototypes are created and experienced by the user, and, based on observation and user feedback, the prototype is reiterated again and again. Rapid prototyping teaches colleagues a "learn by doing" mentality and expedites the process of turning thoughts into actions. As Tom said, "you need to stop talking and start doing."

As you can imagine, this puts a new spin on change management. Change no longer becomes a goal to reach, or a well-defined process. Then, change and ability to deal with change is embedded in the culture of the firm. The technology firms use fuels this continuous change, and because of this the practitioners have more time and space for innovation.

What many old-school firms do not understand is how embracing the four tenets will actually get you additional capacity to do the things you want to do. You can use that additional capacity in order to bring in more work, or you can use those added resources for research and development, creating even more opportunities for growth.

It's this additional capacity that is by far the biggest benefit that firms who embrace an agile mindset reap. When you have capacity it's easier to improve. It's easier to do other things. Capacity allows for more customer work. But it also allows for more innovation-driven product development.

Before this year, 30 percent of my time was technical, 30 percent of my time was operational and 40 percent was media driven. Our firm has five people. There are not many firms my size who operate in that model.

Capitalizing on Capacity:
An Interview with Father/Son Team
Bernard N. Ackerman, CPA/PFS, CFP, CGMA, CDFA
and Jason L. Ackerman CPA, CFP, CGMA of BNA CPA

By Kayleigh Padar

Jason Ackerman and Bernard Ackerman run the firm BNA CPA together as a dynamic family duo. Based in Rock Hill, SC, the firm consists of 20 employees and is modernized, offering flexible schedules to their employees and choosing value pricing over timesheets. "My dad has always had a progressive mindset," said Jason Ackerman. "He has always had the mindset that anybody can contribute to the team and he really focuses on the team culture."

Their change process involves one leader, Bernie, guiding the rest of the team toward a vision of change. There is no group of partners that needs to be convinced every time an adjustment is made. Jason finds that this model means change can happen more quickly.

"Change happens, I think, by somebody in the firm who sees the change and they work on it and then they show other people and it kind of spreads. That's been our model," Jason said.

Despite this form of leadership, employees still have a say in what changes around the office. "We're still run by consensus, we really are." Bernie said.

The first step that the team took to modernize was transitioning to value pricing. Value pricing involves customers paying for work priced up-front rather than time spent.

Another aspect of the firm that is modern is the way employees work within the firm. Employees are thrust into the heart of the firm straight away, and expected to learn through experience. "When you start here, first day, you're working, you'll have direct contact with the clients," Jason said. "There's no seven-year waiting, like 'I'm going to draft an email and forward it to my manager.'"

Along with this immediate inclusion, employees receive an array of benefits. Employees don't need to keep track of hours worked and are able to work from home whenever they choose.

"It's empowering. You have to empower your staff, and they have to feel like they have skin in the game and they're responsible for their clients," Jason said.

They also have almost unlimited off days, as long as the work they are assigned is completed on time. "People come to interview with us and they're amazed because it's just so different from everybody else around us," Jason said.

The Ackermans are confident this system works because there has been no employee turnover or complaints. Clients seem to enjoy this system as well and find that it suits their needs.

"A couple of them [customers] said, "Why hadn't you been doing this 10 years ago?" Bernie said.

The firm has changed for the better since these new implementations were added. "We're a lot more nimble than we were. We can react quicker than we could before because of the technology. We definitely are more on top of our clients than we were because of technology," Bernie said.

This pair would encourage other firms to modernize their practices as well. Specifically, they believe New Firms should focus on client relationships more than the product being sold.

"Firms are going away from the relationship focus. They're going to, 'How many tax returns can we run through our tax return factory and I don't ever want to talk to a client and meet with them.' We're going the exact opposite way," Jason said.

Without this relationship, Jason believes that traditional accounting practices have little value.

"If you don't have the customer relationship, then they're just going to go TurboTax. Eventually the systems are going to be sophisticated enough to where they're going to be able to do their tax returns themselves, so you have to have that relationship and you have to prove your value," Jason said.

But how is it possible for a firm like this to exist? The Ackermans utilize multiple forms of technology in order to keep things running smoothly. For example, the software, Karbon, has been essential to managing everything that is going on in the firm.

"Karbon is how I manage. I have Karbon probably opened up on three different screens all the time looking at where everything is. That was really wonderful for me this tax season," Bernie said.

As for the two Ackermans of the firm, they spend most of their saved time interacting with clients and continuing to reinvent their firm. Change is now just part of their DNA. They are excited about their future.

Tiny steps lead you into the future.

CPAs are busy people. Oftentimes to the detriment of their customers. When CPAs don't have time to understand their customers, they fail to give them real value and creative solutions. This is really concerning to me. It concerns me that many CPAs are unwilling to do the work to keep their firms relevant. Although they know that the world no longer works the way it did 20 years ago, they simply shrug their shoulders or look the other way because confronting change seems like too much work.

> What I'm finding is that these retiring CPAs are not willing to give up their compensation nor their status within a firm in order to make the changes. I've got news: It's highly unlikely that the next generation of CPAs will purchase an old-school firm. It's way easier to open a new online firm, embrace the cloud, and steal clients ready to jump.

The reason? They just don't know where to start. When something becomes overwhelming it's easier to ignore it or look the other way than to try and figure it out. But here's what I think is really creating the problem: succession, older partners and their desire to retire. It will take time, effort, and money to invest in your firm in order to remain relevant—not just today, but for generations to come. That is, if you want your firm to stick around. However, what I'm finding is that these retiring CPAs are not willing to give up their compensation nor their status within a firm in order to make the changes. I've got news: It's highly unlikely that the next generation of CPAs will purchase an old-school firm. It's way easier to open a new online firm, embrace the cloud, and steal clients ready to jump. This is the biggest problem. Many CPAs are just flat out getting outpaced.

Midsized firms, begin here

If you are a midsized firm, you've built your business to where it is today, and you can pivot your business into being more future-ready. Here are 10 steps you can take now to begin the process.
1. Identify the first critical change your firm needs to make and align it to your current business goals. For example, let's use the goal of starting to price up-front a certain service offering. Answer these questions:
    a. What do we need to change. Is it a sales process? A culture? A delivery model? An expectation?

b. Why is this change required? Perhaps it's because others in the marketplace are changing, technology is improving, or there's a better customer service model out there you're not using.
2. Pick a small team to work on this change. When I say small, I mean less than five people. Apply the term "agile" to the team.
   a. Include a young person, a partner who can establish change (aka a decision-maker), a subject matter expert, and someone who is anti-change.
3. Charge the team to create initiatives to support change.
   a. Get super specific here. One bigger goal, made up of lots of little goals.
   b. Create a product based in current services.
   c. Understand the customer.
   d. Understand the choose the technology.
   e. Apply service offering to change-friendly customer.
   f. Learn from any mistakes.
   g. Conduct an after action review.
   h. Alter the solution.
   i. Create pricing.
   j. Train a bigger team on the offering.
   k. Market the solution.
   l. Tie into the sales process.
   m. Embed into the payment process.
4. Set a timeline and define the scope of the change project. Each action step needs a deadline. The team should develop this and facilitate accountability.
5. Define budget for the spend and internal time for each of the action steps.
6. Develop a transparent communication strategy so all your employees know what's happening.
7. Define and provide a support structure for your small team initially and for later to enhance further firm-wide involvement.
8. Iterate, measure, and report back.
   a. Make sure to establish data points—these points should be subjective and non-subjective to measure what success looks like.
9. Don't give up!
10. Celebrate the result—acknowledge the effort involved and whatever positive outcome appears.

Irrelevance is dangerous to your practice. For many Radical CPAs this is an opportunity because we are staying in front of the changes. But for the old-school types, this stagnancy is death. Agile firms will use whatever technology they have to their advantage and watch their growth double organically with ease. I hate to say this, but firms that don't keep up and provide their customers with the best possible solutions could subject themselves to malpractice. When CPAs believe that the world works the same as it did 20 years ago, they don't ask the right questions. By not asking the correct questions, they miss regulatory compliance issues by their own self-limiting thoughts. Nexus applies to exponentially more companies today due to the world of remote work. Just because your firm doesn't allow remote work, doesn't mean the rest of the world is not working remotely with multistate issues and questions aren't being asked.

I'm not trying to scare you into going Radical. Though I clearly think you should. I'm just telling you what you can expect if you don't keep up with technology and innovation and their direct impact on regulatory issues

Think customer experience, not customer service.

Innovation isn't just about the technology you use and how you use it, it's about how you create an experience for your customer. Still, after all this time, CPAs are still unaware that they can create a phenomenal experience around the art of taxes and accounting. I think it's hard for them to imagine the opportunities to serve and delight their customers in a new way. We all know our customers are built on relationships; however, in today's fast moving world, I'm not sure that is enough. The customer's expectations have changed around service models and response times. CPAs need to figure out how to match these ever-expanding expectations.

Innovation isn't just about the technology you use and how you use it, it's about how you create an experience for your customer.

And the expectations don't just belong to the customers. Firm owners have to also meet the needs of employees. Have you checked in with your team lately? We hear the same things over and over: Team members are frustrated and annoyed with the partner group's lack of interest in real change or their ability to grasp what it takes. The problem is, they don't stick around long because it's their market. It's a talent war out there, folks, and the most progressive firms are getting the best of the bunch. The 2016 National Benchmarking Report released by "INSIDE Public Accounting" estimated average turnover at public accounting firms with more than $75 million revenue at 17.2 percent. In addition, in its report on global labor force trends, the McKinsey Global Institute concluded that by 2020 there will be a global supply shortage of 83 -85 million people with college degrees or secondary education.

However, talent will respond to a lower wage if the culture is a good match. Culture is complicated, and later in this book, we'll look at how being a more diverse and inclusive environment can increase retention and improve innovation.

Revolutionizing HR:
An Interview with Brad Self of Clark Schaefer Hackett

By Kayleigh Padar

Brad Self, CPM, Ed.E, MAS is the chief talent officer at the accounting firm Clark Schaefer Hackett. CSH has worked extensively on revolutionizing processes in the HR space. "We wanted to be a firm where people feel like they can come and they are a value," said Self. "They can thrive, they can grow. Our growth model was always, in past years, clients first, but the relationship with our people in the offices always was subpar. For many different reasons. And, the focus was never on our own people, but always on the clients."

That has changed.

CSH has over 400 employees in six locations in Ohio and in Northern Kentucky. Self has had a part in implementing different strategies to retain more employees and increase firm culture.

The firm has a career progression model. In this model, staff have technical and development requirements that need to be fulfilled. The requirements range from communication skills to management skills to interpersonal skills. There are specific courses and programs that address each skill requirement designed into personal growth programs each year.

Everyone is required to have 40 hours of CPE, but the program blends those technical skills with communication skills. This model saves the firm money and helps retain more employees.

"Nobody developed it [the career progression model] out, and we were wasting quite a bit of money because people would come back and say, 'That was over my head,' or 'That was too low,'" Self said. "And now we've got metrics, and we saved literally hundreds of thousands of dollars in trainings."

The shareholders of the firm support this new process wholeheartedly. After all, a top priority was to be appealing to the incoming workforce.

"We were at a place three years ago where the organization was saying, 'Listen, we've... got to change.' There was a large concern that we were going to get gobbled up by the big guys," Self said. "We need to grow organically, and we need to make sure we're engaging our employees, and they feel engaged and valued. And, that's just not the typical mindset as I came into public accounting that was out there."

The message that Self wants to get across to graduating accounting students is that they deserve firms that are willing to help them grow and develop their talents rather than overwork them. "I'd much rather you go to an organization, [wherever] that is, and have somebody invest in your growth and your development, because I'll be honest with you. Young people, I don't want you after you're burnt out. Because I have to relight your fire," Self said.

This message seems to be working. This year, the company overfilled their recruiting pools and was unable to hire the majority of graduates who applied for positions.

Another large focus in this shift is about building relationships within the staff of a company. "I would say from a business model we are much more cognizant of the relationships we have with our teams first before we send them out. I mean, down to the basics. When we construct a team to go to a client, we look at the project's technical requirements and then match the personalities, behaviors, and strengths of the team to the project," Self said.

In fact, Self would argue that relationships are the most important part of a firm's success. "If I could clear all of the things that we've done and get down to couple of things, I would say being very intentional about building relationships is important. Senior leadership was very good about building relationships with clients, but frankly didn't really know where to start with building relationships with the people they work with. Even at a peer level," Self said.

To achieve these goals, the team put together two programs, a coaching program and a mentoring program. The coaches are trained to coach and build relationships with staff. The mentoring program involves every shareholder mentoring a manager. Before, the greatest employee turnover was in the managing pool, but now that rate has gone down.

"We taught our shareholders how to mentor effectively, how to build relationships. And it's been quite transformational for both parties," Self said.

For example, Self suggested that the shareholders begin calling down young employees to their offices to compliment them on hard work and achievements rather than chew them out on poor jobs. This only further benefited the interpersonal relationships in the firms, and caused the entire business to run more smoothly.

"I said, 'Guys, you influence these young people every day. That's what leadership is, not about your title, but about your ability to influence people. And you can influence them in a positive or negative way,'" Self said.

In the past year, employees of CSH have been traveling and speaking to different accounting firms to share their new methods to benefit others.

"We really believe that leadership is influence. And you have an opportunity to influence people you come into contact with in a positive or negative way, and that influence directly relates to your ability to be able to lead. People want to follow you; they don't have to follow you," Self said.

Understanding the urgency behind the intersection of user experience, technology, and business.

We've talked about innovation. It's not going away. We've talked about the importance of having an agile mindset, and more of us are illustrating that in the way we run our firms. And you also by now are familiar with the four (okay, five) tenets that are the foundation of a Radical firm. But let's talk about accounting transformation. Let's talk about the crossroads of user experience (UX), technology, and business.

Somehow, they are all intersecting and we're not exactly sure what to do. When I say we're not exactly sure, the Radicals are working on it, and we're figuring it out, but there is a long way for us to go.

Why?

Because we don't even have the tools that we need to service our customers properly. The profession's legacy vendors have not kept up with the Internet of things (IoT) technology and user expectations, because of our profession's slow adoption. The Internet companies that aren't firms are scaling faster, cheaper, and sexier than traditional firms. And VC capital is funding the technology, experience, and business. Smaller agile firms desperately want the vendors in the space to move faster.

Our customers aren't exactly sure how to use our new technologies. Think about it: We've used portals for a long time now, but are portals the most user-friendly experience in the world? Nope! How do we combine the two? How do we merge the offline and the online worlds together to make it so that everybody loves what's happening? So, we truly have that cross-section of user experience technology in our CPA firm and with our customers—and they are all working together nicely?

Remember that old-school ketchup bottle I talked about in *The Radical CPA* illustrating the old-school firm, you know where you're shaking and trying to get the information out and it's taking forever? In cloud-based firms, the technology firms are the latest cutting edge ketchup bottle—where it's easy to squeeze and get what you want right away. You can even take it one step further with a ketchup packet from your favorite fast food joint. You can tear it open or open from the top to dip. My point? The customer has a choice for ketchup delivery.

How can we transition our firms to be like a key with... no key? In the old days, cars had keys and you had to turn the ignition to start a car, right? Many cars now have key fobs that just need to be in the vicinity of the car to start it. And today you can start a car with an app from your phone!

How will we deliver data in similar ways?

Think about it like this: Right now, CPAs are the key to the data. But now the question is, how can we have the information make an impact without a report? I don't know the answer but I know we will have to create a solution soon.

How Blinders Hurt Clients

> I truly believe CPAs think they are serving their customers well, but their blinders prevent them from being exceptional.

As a Radical CPA, or as a managing partner of a wannabe Radical CPA firm, you are already up for the challenge. Our job is to get others to join us! I don't think they really understand the urgency of the Radical manifesto. Tax seasons come and go, and if they see some minimal growth and their team doesn't leave in an exodus, they're fine. But that's no way to run a business. I truly believe CPAs think they are serving their customers well, but their blinders prevent them from being exceptional. There is nothing like feeling the fear, walking through the confusion, and making it out more successful than ever before. If we've been through it, it's more likely our customers will trust us when they must go through it themselves. When customers are expecting digital transformation and we haven't been through that transformation, why should they come to us to guide them?

CHAPTER 3

Firm Product Management is the Way to the Future

What is your firm's purpose?

Let's go back to the idea of innovation, or what I like to describe as the application of innovation and business model transformation.

We're not just managing change anymore. Change management is becoming obsolete—New Firms know they must be nimbler than just strategizing around any sort of targeted change. Managing change was fine five years ago, but trust me when I say we are beyond that.

What I've realized is that firm management is evolving into product management.

Now hear me out, before you think I'm throwing service out the window.

Product management is what technology companies do when they create new technology. It's the organizational lifecycle dealing with the planning, the forecasting, the production, and the marketing of a product or products in all its stages.

If you look at this definition from Wikipedia, product management "integrates people, data, process, and business systems." Isn't that what we do as CPAs?

I mean, think about it. Don't we integrate people, data, process, and business systems? Don't we do this to provide the best service possible to our customers?

It's a brain change. We haven't before thought of ourselves as a product. We always think of ourselves as selling service hours, but if you move to fixed pricing, or a value-pricing model, we're in a whole different ballgame. We're selling a product now and really a result or even transformation. It's like what Ron Baker of VeraSage Institute said, "The customers become the product in a transformation."

The question becomes, how are we going to keep that product innovative and cutting-edge so that we're not just selling service hours? Because, guess what? We shouldn't be thinking of ourselves as selling service hours anymore.

In a traditional CPA firm, most deals are structured on a combination of time and scope. As the scope of requirements increases, so does the time needed to deliver them, so the price goes up. In other words, the more work the customer wants done, the more they'll have to pay. In this situation, the customer is incentivized to ask for less, while the firm is incentivized to find more work for more billing.

A productized service is organized differently. It's designed to align the incentives of both the provider and the customer around one common purpose: To produce desirable results for the customer.

Case Study:
Launching a New Product Line at New Vision, New Vision Wealth Management

The best way to explain how this works is to talk about a new product launch at my firm. We are in the process of launching wealth management services, and we are doing it via a product management model.

How did we decide we wanted to do this? It was the next natural step.

Our customers were asking us about financial planning.

I also saw some of our younger business owners exit their companies and watched their wealth leave our firm because we were no longer able to meet their needs.

I decided it was time to get licensed.

Not to mention, a shift of generational wealth is starting to occur as the baby boomers are dying and my customer base is primed to receive inheritances.

I also believe that complete financial planning should be in a firm. It just makes sense to serve your customer from a holistic point of view. If you look at any of the bigger firms, they offer wealth management as it is a complementary offering.

Perhaps even most importantly, fintech helps us provide services that our cloud-based customers expect. We are a technology-driven firm and now, thanks to the latest in financial technology, we can meet them where they are online.

Once again, traditional CPA financial planning firm owners are not meeting the needs of the next generation of customers, when they expect in-person face-to-face meetings.

Now, I know compliance is tough and it's not as easy to transact using the Internet, but I've trail blazed before. Why shouldn't CPA financial planners be able to serve their customers in the same fintech driven way?

Where did we start?

We decided to align with 1st Global, which only serves CPA firm owners. They are our RIA and our broker dealer.

Why 1st Global?

After doing research and asking other firms we knew, we did not want to be an in-house RIA. We also knew we wanted to have a complete offering as we got more involved in the financial planning space.

Also, I challenged their leadership team about where I wanted to be from a fintech perspective, and they were open to be challenged. It started with compliance doing a social media audit of me. Talk about walking into an unusual relationship!

We created a business plan using Aha!. We defined what we would sell. This is a big deal because we didn't just say we would sell everything 1st Global offers. We defined a handful of products that we believed would complement our current customers' needs. We don't want to be everything to everybody, and are comfortable with defining who we want to serve and how we will serve them. That means we may turn down business because it does not fit into our product line offering.

The slide below is a one-page overview of what we are selling and who we are selling to. It can keep our whole firm engaged with a simple explanation of our new product line goals. This is especially helpful for the members of our team who are not directly involved in the initiative.

Description			Key Objectives		
Cloud-based Wealth Management • Based in Cash Planning/Budgeting • IMS Platform for securities			1. To become the one stop firm for complete accounting, tax, and financial services. 2. $30 million in assets within 3 years.		
Customer Targets	**Customer Challenges**	**Our Solution**	**Our Value**	**Our Pricing**	
Types of customers who purchase your solution 1. Current Accounting Small Business Customers 2. Jim's Tax Customers	1. Not sure where to go/who to trust 2. Web-based solutions are intriguing, especially big brands. 3. Know enough to be dangerous	They already trust us. Already in their financial underwear drawer. One stop shop	We have the complete financial picture We live and already love the cloud and the increased communication/real-time chaos it brings We are not selling product but here for the long term We already have a fiduciary responsibility	Financial Planning as a fixed fee service Financial Planning as part of assets under management $1 million or less – 1.3% Above $1 million – 1% Above $10 million – Custom *Fee Only* Net Income & Net Assets <$250,000 – $3,000 Net Income & Net Assets <$500,000 – $4,500 Net Income & Net Assets >$1,000,000 – $6,000 Above $1,000,000 – Custom	
Our Messaging			**Go-to-Market**		
Clear and compelling message that explains why your solution is worth buying Your BFF – Best Business Friend Clear understanding of your complete financial picture with the ability to piggy back long term as well as short term financial goals.			Channels used to market and sell to your customers E-money as a free giveaway tp all our current customers Financial Planning as a fixed fee service Financial Planning as part of assets under management		
Investment Requirement			**Growth Opportunity**		
Costs required to make the solution a success Education Learning Curve About $1,000 per month technology/fees			Ways that you will grow the business Stickiness and loyalty, and love to create more referrals Promote/Promote/Promote Utilize technology to fuel growth		

Business model for New Vision Wealth Management (Template via aha.io)

Chart: Value vs. Effort

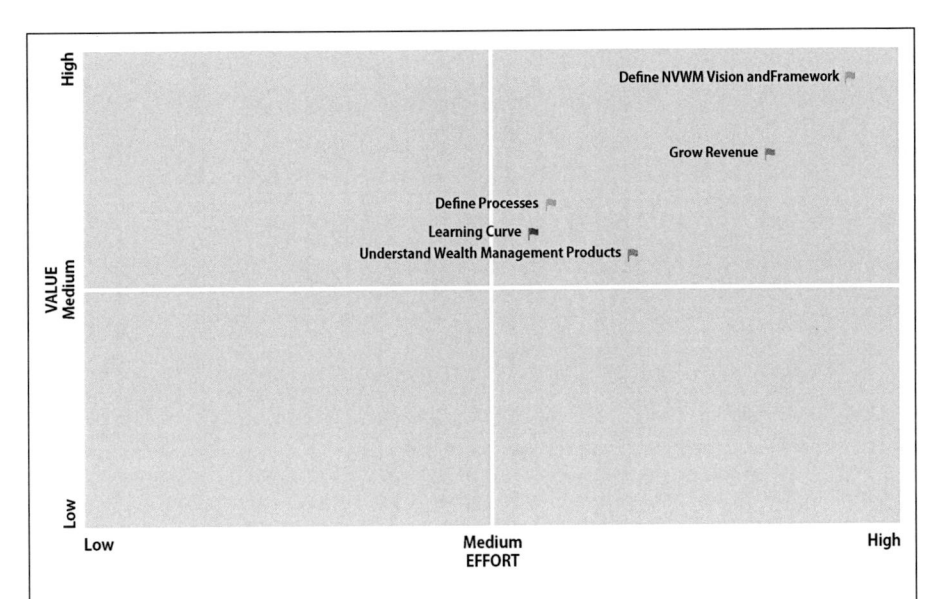

Y-axis: VALUE (Low, Medium, High)
X-axis: EFFORT (Low, Medium, High)

- Define NVWM Vision and Framework — High Value, High Effort
- Grow Revenue — High Value, High Effort
- Define Processes — Medium Value, Medium Effort
- Learning Curve — Medium Value, Medium Effort
- Understand Wealth Management Products — Medium Value, Medium Effort

Goals for New Vision Wealth Management

When you can create goals that are important to your product line, it simplifies your thought process on how to implement them. The above chart is my top-of-mind picture to remind me and the firm what of what's important. This is what our wealth management team will be working towards every day, and everyone knows it.

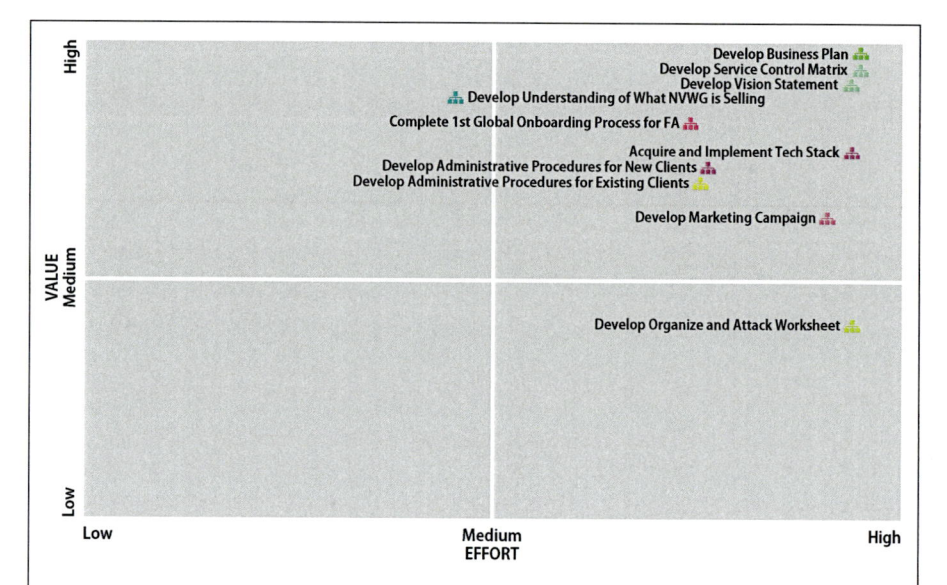

```
                                                          Develop Business Plan
                                                       Develop Service Control Matrix
High                                                     Develop Vision Statement
                                       Develop Understanding of What NVWG is Selling
                                  Complete 1st Global Onboarding Process for FA
                                                     Acquire and Implement Tech Stack
                                 Develop Administrative Procedures for New Clients
                                 Develop Administrative Procedures for Existing Clients
VALUE
Medium                                                    Develop Marketing Campaign


                                                     Develop Organize and Attack Worksheet


Low
       Low                              Medium                                    High
                                        EFFORT
```

Initiatives for New Vision Wealth Management

The above shows the initiatives that help our firm achieve our four goals. These initiatives begin to give us boundaries and structure to allow us to implement our bigger goals.

And so begins our roadmap for this specific product line.

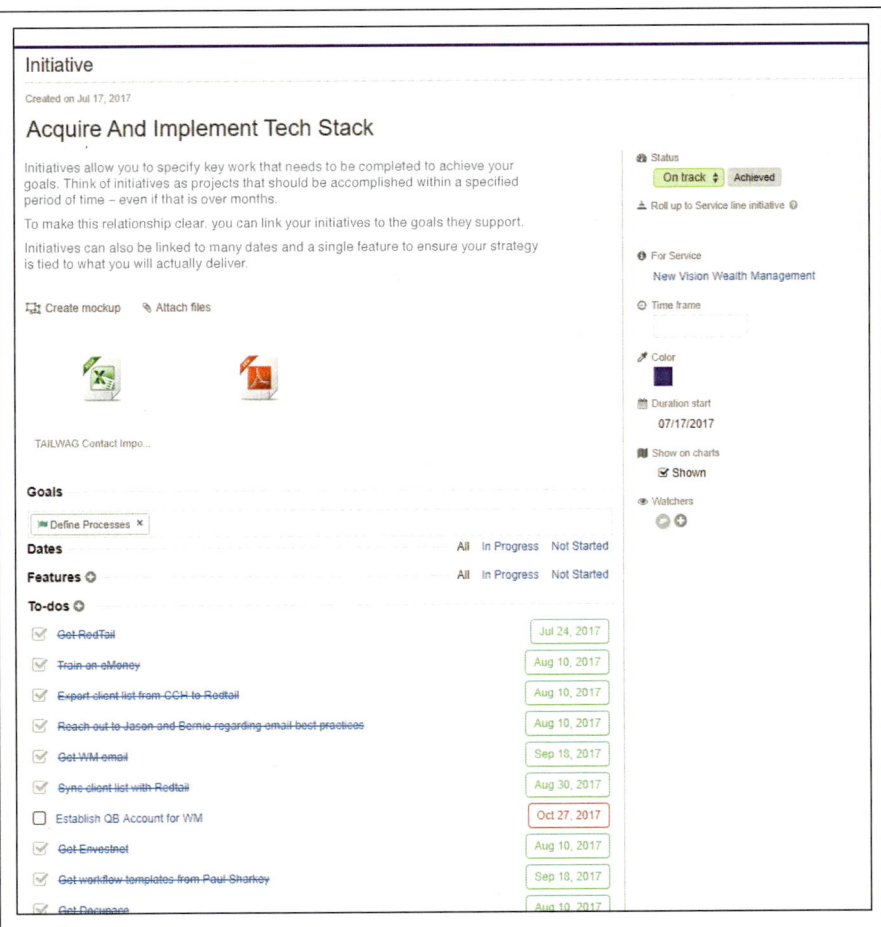

Specific Initiatives: A Set of Specific Tasks to Accomplish for New Vision Wealth Management (Via aha.io)

This specific feature applies to Define Process. Now everything just becomes a to-do with defined and accountable dates for completion.

See how it becomes much easier for everyone to work toward a common outcome? It shows us that it's not this big behemoth of change, but an opportunity to just do work.

When you can clearly define a product line and its offering, it just becomes easier for all involved. Everyone knows their roles, their objectives and the to-dos to get there.

I am not naive to think we won't have different iterations as we launch and

> learn from our customers and ourselves. However, when the whole team has a complete understanding of what is happening and the steps to get there, and an understanding that we will iterate all the way, it makes for a happier team.

OKAY. But how do we do this?

The short answer? Technology.

One of the tools that I use is Aha!. Technically, it's marketed as product roadmap software. But I use it for so much more. It helps me flesh out my vision and strategy while also helping my team and me track our activities day to day. It's how I manage our firm so that we have accountability for all the change and innovation that we experience.

Process updating no longer works. Updating your process does not help with selling something other than time. We must think about process in relationship to the products we are now selling. Stop thinking process and start thinking products composed of process, people, data, and a result. Product management will help you manage your firm like the boss you are!

This has been one of the biggest "aha moments" for me.

No pun intended.

I've seen it happen time and time again with new software products that vendors have created for our firms. It starts with the CPA getting all excited about the tech. You know how it rolls out: "Yes, this is a problem," says the CPA, "and I think this software can help my customer." The CPA signs up for the trial. Then it stops there. A year later, the CPA isn't using it and you can bet none of the CPA's customers are using it. Yet, if this vendor goes directly to the CPA's customer with the product and it gets adopted, the CPA feels jilted.

And yes, sometimes that happens. In fact, it's happening more and more.

Then what? The CPA is out of the loop. And we know once that takes place, the stickiness of the customer to that CPA becomes, well, unstuck.

Here's my solution to that issue. A solution, I think, will be what we need to do to stay relevant for our customers:

First things first: Let's first stop.

Let's pause and figure out the actual value of the tool attached to the value that we as CPAs bring to the table.

Then let's create a solution with the software tool, the CPA, the process, and the data collection and create a complete product solution . . . not just a software implementation.

Finally, we market this as one solution specifically directed to a specific market or niche.

We have the wrong idea on how to implement new tools today. We've been having a hard time developing a solution that can really help us get closer to our customers.

We need to step back and create a "productized service" for each new technology or service that gives us a complete result we choose to implement.

This productized service needs to be for a specific customer as well. It must be customized yet standardized so that it is so perfect for a specific customer that it easily scales across that customer base. In our firms today, little is standardized, or even customized with intention. It's just a haphazard approach of different software and services.

We need to strategically think about the end user (customer), our price, our roll-out, our value-add, our marketing, and, most importantly, why our customer or a prospect could and would purchase this solution from us.

Firms have tried "solution selling," but really that is just a renamed version of selling time. They never really created a solution; they just promoted it differently. That needs to stop now. So, now we have a productized service. That's what we have done with the outsourced accounting services model. But we need to do it at a much more specific level. We need to get into the detail of everything we potentially sell. And if we can't figure out how to sell it without an hourly price around it, I would challenge you to answer this question honestly: Is it in the best interest of our customer to sell this, or should we refer out to another firm with that specialization?

How to Create a Productized Service In its Simplest Form

- Define customer
- Define outputs and scope
- Define scope creep and seep so you know what and where it could happen. What makes it out of scope and what is a newly-priced option?
- Define costs
- Determine price
- Package and market

1099s as a Productized Service

Here's how I took a really easy service many of us provide and turned it into a product using the above list.

Define Customer
- Small business owner, up to $10 million gross receipts
- Uses cloud accounting
- Has subcontractors

Define Outputs and Scope
- Needs 1099s filed electronically. Allow only one way. Paper filings are exceptions for extreme cases. If you want to paper file, we won't do it
- 1099 information collected before subcontractor gets paid
- We provide system, customer may or may not have us involved with actual payment processing

Define Costs
- Intuit online payroll software
- Team labor for setup
- Team labor training
- Team labor if electronic payments processed. We only allow electronic payments. No other choices
- Team labor e-filing/mailing in January

Determine Price
- How many contractors used over course of year

- Price changes based on inputs/value to customer

Package and Market
- Included as part of our small business complete solution
- Typically not sold as its own package
- If not right fit for our process, we refer elsewhere. It's OK for us not to provide this service. They can do them internally or go elsewhere

Productizing a Core Service the New Vision Way: How 1099s are Filed at My Firm

Here's the old-school way of completing 1099s:

CPA calls customer before year-end reminding them 1099s need to be completed for January. CPA reminds customer to send in names, addresses, and amounts for 1099s to be issued. CPA waits for complete data, usually missing at least one address. CPA rushes at last minute to enter data in 1099 system and issue 1099s. CPAs have multiple customers who act like this, creating havoc and late nights in January.

It doesn't have to be this way!

Many people ask me how we file 1099s. The biggest tip I give people is that there is only one way we do this. We don't allow our customers to pay and file 1099s haphazardly. They are required to follow the rules, guidelines, and system that we provide. We've found this to be the most successful.
- All our customers are on Intuit Payroll for Accountants
- All our customers must use this system to pay contractors
- At the end of year, we confirm payments were made via Intuit Payroll for Accountants
- Print, mail, and e-file only 1099s
- All created and filed by second week of January

You don't have to do our exact system of 1099s to be successful; however, when the outside regulatory dates changed this year, our system didn't miss a beat. Why? Because we had a process that our customers followed. They had to play by our rules.

1099s prepared the way we do takes us minutes, not hours.

We file hundreds of 1099s in a day.

When we onboard a small business, we ask them about potential contractors. We tell them about how the payments and the process will work. We teach them the software, and we do this all during the year, not at the last minute.

Small business owners adapt to our system, allowing us to build in capacity. This is why process and technology are so important.

We don't give these small businesses a chance to tell us how they are going to do it. We give them a system that works.

We sold a productized solution of 1099s. If they don't want to use our service, no worries, we just won't prepare their 1099s. We have higher value work that needs to be done in January. We don't want to be focusing on an administrative function because we don't want to wear out our team. Also, because our year-ends are already done, we can start business tax returns as soon as the software is ready.

We need to create productized services for everything. For how we sell and support payroll, accounting, tax, for benchmarking and dashboards, for forecasting, for the sale of a business, and yes, I think we can even do it for IRS resolution.

All those things we used to sell at an hourly rate? We need to now create a process that includes tools, labor, and pricing. It's an all-inclusive package, so to speak.

When we do this, we can get our whole team understanding what we sell, how we deliver it, and their part in the process/product. We can become a more efficient and effective firm. Team members will also become better at selling because they completely understand the result. It's hard to sell something that doesn't have closure. It's easier to sell a result or solution.

This is why many midsized firms are having a hard time moving away from the hourly model. They haven't redefined their paradigm. They haven't thought of themselves as product managers.

Product Management: Let's Go Deeper

If we are going to be acting like product managers, we really need to know what they do. The best place to start is defining product management.

According to Steven Haines' book, The Product Manager's Survival Guide, product management refers to the holistic management of products and portfolios—from the time they are conceived to the time they are discontinued and withdrawn from the market. In essence, it's the business management of products. Product management can also refer to the organization that serves to lead and integrate the work of people from other functions.

That said, a product manager is a person appointed to be the proactive manager of a product or a product line. They resemble a CEO or a general manager because these people are best equipped to guide organizations and lead cross-functional product teams. This is why smaller firms can productize their service line offerings much faster than the larger firms. Their teams are smaller and their partners come to the table with the mindset of acting liking a startup CPA firm. Their partners take on the CEO role, instead of being stuck in the position of focusing on billable hours or technical work. They run their firms like a business, not like traditional professional services firm partnerships.

Many CPAs have functional mindsets and will have to recondition themselves to work in this in a new way.

I find it exciting.

And no, not everyone needs to be a product manager or have that set of skills. But I bet someone from your team is just plumb perfect for the position.

Monster.com Product Manager Job Description

Product manager skills and qualifications:
- Product management
- People management

- Product development
- Understanding the customer
- Requirements analysis
- Competitive analysis
- Pricing
- Planning
- Sales planning
- Financial planning and strategy
- Inventory control

Product manager job responsibilities:
- Develops products by identifying potential products
- Conducts market research
- Generates product requirements
- Determines specifications, production timetables, pricing, and time-integrated plans for product introduction
- Develops marketing strategies

Product manager job duties:
- Determines customers' needs and desires by specifying the research needed to obtain market information
- Recommends the nature and scope of present and future product lines by reviewing product specifications and requirements; appraises new product ideas and/or product or packaging changes
- Assesses market competition by comparing the company's product to competitors' products
- Provides source data for product line communications by defining product marketing communication objectives
- Obtains product market share by working with sales director to develop product sales strategies
- Assesses product market data by calling on customers with field salespeople and evaluating sales call results
- Provides information for management by preparing short-term and long-term product sales forecasts and special reports and analyses; answers questions and requests
- Facilitates inventory turnover and product availability by reviewing and adjusting inventory levels and production schedules
- Brings new products to market by: analyzing proposed product requirements and product development programs; preparing return on investment analyses;

- establishing time schedules with engineering and manufacturing
- Introduces and markets new products by developing time-integrated plans with sales, advertising, and production
- Determines product pricing by: utilizing market research data; reviewing production and sales costs; anticipating volume; costing special and customized orders
- Completes operational requirements by scheduling and assigning employees; follows up on work results
- Maintains product management staff by recruiting, selecting, orienting, and training employees
- Maintains product management staff job results by counseling and disciplining employees, planning, monitoring, and appraising job results
- Maintains professional and technical knowledge by: attending educational workshops; reviewing professional publications; establishing personal networks; participating in professional societies
- Contributes to team effort by accomplishing related results as needed

To be successful in product management, you need a variety of skills.

You must have the ability to look up and down and across the organization to build a cross-functional mindset within your culture. No one will become the perfect product manager overnight; however, if you can follow the blueprint in this chapter you'll have a running start. Your success will be built on how fast you get up off the ground to achieve early noticeable wins.

A product manager works across the whole organization. Firms today, as well as many large businesses, are still so siloed in their approaches. This person figures out the way to for them to work together toward a common product or solution. If the product manager is successful, there will most likely be a strong financial return—which as you know, makes everyone look good!

Tips From a Veteran Product Manager

By Bill Whitson

In my 20-plus years in the tax, accounting, and finance world, I've learned a few things along the way. I'll share some from the product management lens.

Product managers can be, in many ways, like trusted advisors: They have a strong opinion, an extensive toolkit, and they serve nearly everyone around them.

Opinions Versus Data

The key difference in the statement above is that for a product manager, their opinion is not that important. In fact, it can be their worst enemy. This takes me to my first training recommendation and quote:

"While your opinion may be interesting, it is not important." —Pragmatic Marketing

This is something they teach in the highly praised Pragmatic Marketing program, and it's a hard pill to swallow for many. A strong opinion is usually accompanied by a high degree of "tribal knowledge," which can be as equally destructive. While tribal knowledge has its place as a data point, it's only one data point.

Other traits shared by successful advisors and product managers are keen observation and effective listening skills, which go hand-in-hand in data collection. Observation is far more powerful for uncovering needs and finding pain points, but listening seems to be more emphasized—aka the "voice of the customer." Yes, listening is important but there are a couple of traps to be wary of. First, many times customers tell you what they want you to hear, in a way that might lead you to solve for their agenda. They don't always represent your target customer or the rest of your customer base. Customers also tend to derive perceived solutions and may bias your discovery because it can appear there is an easy answer on how you should proceed. "Solutioneering" can also happen during brainstorming sessions led by highly opinionated product managers. Secondly, listening to the market is equally important as listening to individuals. The market represents the collective voice of who will buy your product or service, and this voice represents the growth that every business owner is looking for.

On the other hand, observation allows you to get a firsthand account of how your customer consumes or uses your product/solution. You'll also learn that many times what a customer says contradicts how they actually behave. This is referred to as the "say/do ratio." Having spent 16 years at Intuit, it was ingrained in our DNA to find ways to observe customers using our solutions in their own habitat. Intuit's founder, Scott Cook, was the first to pioneer the "follow me home" initiative. Google it. And come up with your own version. You'll find you learn exponentially more from observation.

The Toolkit

Once you've mastered observing and listening (can that ever really happen?), you'll need some other tools to assist you in turning all that marvelous data into useful information, help you develop a product strategy, and work with development teams on your product roadmap. Like many trusted advisors, developing an extensive toolkit takes place over time, through trial and error. Some things work better than others in some situations (or organizations) and some don't. Experiment and iterate. There's no one right way.

Here are some thoughts on some great approaches to have in your toolkit:
- As previously noted, find ways to improve your observation and listening skills, and flex these muscles often. Only then will your opinion become valuable to others, because it will reflect the data behind it.
- Also, as previously noted, Pragmatic Marketing is a great program. After you get certified, you get alumni access to all kinds of resources. This is Product Management 101 for any aspiring product manager or anyone else taking a product or solution to market.
- SAFe: Understanding the scaled agile framework is important, if you are in software/app development. Don't feel beholden to the Agile framework—just take the parts that make the most sense for your organization and develop a process that continuously adds value to your product or service.
- Understand the value of UX and user-centered design. Check out UXmatters.com.
- The Product Plan blog is fantastic. Like most blogs, there are subtle plugs for their solution (which is great if you can allocate spend on a roadmap tool), but the articles are spot on and full of tips and other goodies.
- Find a mentor. Have coffee, breakfast, adult beverages. Trade ideas and learn from each other.

Bill Whitson is Sr. Product Manager at RealPage, Inc.

But how does product management work in an accounting firm? (Hint, it's hooked into strategy.)

The product manager in a CPA firm is the leader in developing new products that complement the firm's strategy.

Therefore, you must know your firm's strategy for this person to be successful.

This role works closely with all department heads: technical accounting and tax, technology, practice leaders, marketing, and R&D, always with the customer expectation in mind, to ultimately create a solution to solve and impact the end user.

Here's the kicker: It may or may not be a CPA. The person just really needs to understand the market. Most product managers in technology are not engineers but business people.

Why can't we bring business people to accounting firms? It seems to me that in firms today, the MBA is needed as much as a MSA or MST.

But more importantly, someone at your firm just may naturally have the skillset to be that product manager. Do you know who they are?

We know strategy is important. We also know that the person needs to have an exceptional understanding of the market, so much so that they surpass market expectations. They also must have a love for technology, but aren't the "IT guy." This is a person who is just naturally attracted to all the latest in technology, because we must consider the emergence and evolution of AI, IoT, and other new technologies as you build them into your firm.

"Encouraging CPAs to think like product companies is spot-on because you'll be able to just embed all this technology into your service and really differentiate in the market," said Nick Goode, executive VP of product at Sage.

"Figure out what is going to be general, basic usage of artificial intelligence in the world or in small businesses or business customers," he said. "Then figure out, 'What can I leverage from that technology?' Build a roadmap of services that [you] can deliver to [your] clients. The cut-off point for me has to be anything that can't be completely automated and that they can do on their own or figure out on their own."

Strategy is all year long.

CPAs are familiar with strategy; many firms have created three- or five-year plans at their firm retreats, in between rounds of golf.

But what we're talking about is much bigger than a retreat. This is not a once-a-year process. Strategy needs to be ongoing, so much so that it's baked into your DNA. Connecting your firm's goals and initiatives back to your product management should be representative of your strategy.

After all, we all know the story of the poor strategic plan. You gear up for your partner retreat and pump out a plan, and then you go back to your firm, where the plan becomes a static file on your desktop or an outdated PDF on your Intranet, and/or gets placed in your firm administrator's filing cabinet. You had good intentions, but you know, you have customers to focus your energy. And implementation and execution is so hard!

If you use something like Aha!, you can manage your firm and your products and keep that fluid accountability going. The document becomes a living, recurring event process with built-in accountability. You can use this at weekly, monthly, or quarterly meetings to prioritize which changes and innovation need to happen in your firm. You can put timelines around activities and priorities. This is different than a five-year plan, because, let's face it, you can't wait five years anymore. In fact, I don't even think sometimes we can wait until after tax season. Innovation is happening so quickly now that we need to at least have it on our radar. We can't just plan off-season. We need to make sure during tax season, change is happening, too.

From Practice Management to Product Management

What is fun for me about being part of this (growing) Radical CPA movement is that our firms can all look different from each other. And that we keep evolving.

That said, I have noticed a somewhat disturbing trend among cloud accountants—which makes sense to me since we are still new at this—there are many New Firms who use the same cloud-based fixed price model. So even though it's Radical to be in the cloud in the first place, there is a mimicking of models that feels static. While yes, we should share our resources and how we do things, we must remember that if your firm looks like your competitor's or peer's, that's not necessarily innovation or differentiation.

And we all know how differentiation is a pain point for CPA firms.

There is a fine balance here, and it will be interesting to see how it all evolves over time. Moving over to a product management methodology allows you to iterate all the time so you don't look like every other firm out there.

Most of you would never take a trip without an itinerary or a map, but I'm pretty much asking you to do just that. It's going to be a new role for you to learn how to become a product manager and you're going to start this job without a clear idea of what you are doing.

Sound familiar?

Get used to that feeling! However, the one thing all product people share is that they gained their knowledge and experience from both passed opportunities and serendipity. In other words, they did it despite not having a blueprint to guide them.

I always say I figured this out despite myself. I did it while having no formal background in product management. I was just a CPA with a Master in Taxation. You can do it, too.

Let's do this.

Are you ready to take the plunge? As a Radical CPA, you're already used to dealing with change.

But I'm here to tell you, your customers (and the market) are demanding that you not only deal with change, but master it. So how do you start?

Make a leap of faith. And then deal with the consequences.

First you must make the conscious decision that you are going to start running your firm from a product management perspective.

Once you make that decision you are going to confront many challenges.

You're going to be overwhelmed.

You're going to doubt yourself.

You're going to be frustrated.

It's all normal.

In fact, let's get the three main challenges you'll face right out of the way:

- You have organizational obstacles you don't know how to overcome. You're visualizing your seven other partners not buying into your changes and it makes you want to get into your bed.

- You get caught in the day-to-day and don't have enough time to do the strategic planning needed.
- You feel that your prior experience of preparing tax returns, creating review points, and billing time have not left you well prepared for this new role.

Okay, so now that we've articulated those obstacles, don't you feel better?

Are you going to let it stop you? No!

Now you've made the decision. You're changing your firm to work from a practice management perspective to a product management perspective. So, what do you do first?

The Game Plan

First thing first, get your bearings. I believe (and I've been told) the hardest thing about being a Radical CPA is that there has been no roadmap! Everyone wants a checklist because that's how we were raised in the old-school model. Or they want the perfect firm in a box that they can copy. I'm here to tell you there is no turnkey solution. Yes, we have processes. Yes, we have best practices. But the world is changing too fast for a checklist. In fact, to be frank, there isn't a checklist that exists. However, there are some essentials to help you get there. We have ideas, we have tried and true methodologies, and we have each other's support to create a structure around navigating this complex business environment. The art of product management has been around for years. There are even online courses you can take to master this skill.

It starts with your vision, which I think most people already get. You know you must articulate your vision, your mission, your weaknesses, your strengths, your opportunities. Most of you could do this within your own firms. Every consultant reading this will hate me, but I strongly believe you can do this on your own if you set aside time and find someone on your team willing to spearhead it. You need someone to say, "OK, I'm going to work through this all the time, and this is going to be the way we manage innovation and change in our firm."

I'm going to share with you what I've learned and what I've seen work for others like me. It's not perfect, and it's changing, but I truly believe if you start here you'll end up closer to your desired outcome.

Assess your organization. Go ahead, take a good, long, hard look. Before you can start developing anything, you must figure out how your organization is defined. Is it defined by a chart, or are there unwritten rules as to who is in charge? For instance, there may be a managing partner in a firm, but there may be an unspoken understanding that it's the managing partner's office manager who makes all the decisions. Who in your firm has strong interpersonal skills? What are your team's strengths and weaknesses? Have you done a SWOT analysis? We know that being a leader in a firm today is more than just technical knowledge.

The skill set below is for the person who is going to lead this endeavor. In small firms, this will likely be the partner in charge; in large firms it will be multiple people. I also recommend bringing on an outside person who is not a technical accounting professional, such as someone with general business background who understands the marketplace. It must be someone with a strong understanding of business, not just accounting or tax.

Refer to the skill and qualifications list provided by Monster.com on page 65, and consider the following skill sets and questions when you are doing your internal assessment. Who in your firm has the following skills?

Critical thinking. Is there a person who can continually assimilate and evaluate business, market, financial, and environmental data that leads to important conclusions? Who on your team is brilliant at strategy? Who really knows how to identify opportunities in new places?

Systemic thinking. Who in your firm can make sense of challenging situations and develop simple interventions for transforming them? Are they able to see the patterns that emerge quickly and then come up with creative solutions quickly? Can they see the whole picture? Who is the best at this on your team?

Problem-solving. Who in your firm has a process for assessing any situation that may arise? Are they asking the right questions? Can they evaluate the environment, even as it changes? Have they developed a logical analysis to determine the root cause of the problem? How do they engage others in the analysis and the identification of solutions? Who comes to you with the solution—not another problem—and uses non-traditional thinking to get there?

Strategic thinking. Who in your firm is developing strategies today in uncertain or ambiguous market environments? Can they consider and evaluate various continuous inputs in situations to envision and create future solutions that drive business or product line options? Do you have someone who comes to you with a technology product and tells you the full implementation, not just, "We should sell this?" Who is the person in your firm who can see the future the strongest? Who looks at something challenging and offers up a plan of action?

Next Step: mapping & documentation!

Now that the assessment is complete, we are going to take all that research and those findings and document them. We're then going to decide who our first potential product manager could be and see if they are up for the job.

Is it by chance you?

If so, congratulations on your new role!

But before you pop that champagne bottle, you have work to do.

You must change your brain!

You're a product manager now. You need to understand the characteristics of your new role. You need to see the landscape of the industries you serve and the technologies that will best suit them. This can be the hardest part; however, access to information has never been easier. Do research. Get on Twitter (my favorite way to stay updated on news and trends). Make sure you start to define and sift through all the information coming your way. Welcome to your new job.

> **Product Management: Start Here**
>
> So, you're in your new role. Now what? It's time to get organized and start rolling your plans out to the team. Here are the first steps to take in your new position as product manager.

Develop an organizational chart. Create a visual representation of who's who in your firm and the roles they serve. This will be a key reference for you as you move forward—plus it's nice to get fancy with it and put it up where everyone in the office can see. If you have virtual employees, put it somewhere that is easily accessible, or use it as a screen saver!

Create a roadmap. This is a living, breathing document that includes your firm's priorities and accountability system. Once you do this, you're going to love it, I promise. You could hire a consultant to do this, or you could do it yourself with your team. Back in the day we used to call this strategic planning. Now we're building a business model with an emphasis on product management. And guess what? Our CPA services are the product. Let that sink in.

Know your customer. This may seem obvious, and maybe you're even sick of hearing it. But the truth is, many CPAs never really needed to know and understand their customers in the old-school firm model. We knew what it was we sold, but we tried to sell it to every customer that looked our way. Now, we're taking the time to know our customers and create something special for them. It's time to realize that our customers are more sophisticated and have buying power. They don't have to continue to come to you just because their mom or dad did. Location no longer matters. They will find someone more suited to their needs. Believe me when I say that it's crucial you find out what your customer wants and needs, how they consume their information, how they like to communicate, what their values are, how they spend their time. Knowing all this will help you come up with services and products that make their life easier. Because ultimately, that's what our customers want, right? They want it to be easy and they want to save and grow their money. Do you ask your customers these questions? For example, I always talk about how I use Skype regularly, and old-school firm owners freak out saying their customers would never do that. Really? Have you asked them?

Many CPAs never really needed to know and understand their customers in the old-school firm model. We knew what it was we sold, but we tried to sell it to every customer that looked our way. Now, we're taking the time to know our customers and create something special for them.

Create customer personas. This is about hyper-specializing. This is about marketing to and serving your customers the best possible impact to transform their lives. Once you figure out how you are going to productize your services, think about the customers you are going to serve. It's time to get specific. People always talk about niches, but a lot of people don't really understand them. You can go through your firm, and you can define what your typical customer looks like without necessarily even saying, "okay, my niche is medical practice." But this is more of a proactive approach. This is about the customers who aren't your customers yet. At New Vision, we looked at about 10 or so personalities of our current customer base and created personas around them. What is a persona, you ask? It's fleshing out a person's preferences, lifestyle, and any other identifying characteristics that describe who they are and what they value. Typically, my elevator speech is, "Okay, we serve small business owners, zero to $10 million." What does a small business owner look like in our zero to $10 million range? They vary, but are specific. Our personas are different than saying, "Okay, we take everyone who walks in the door." Our personas dictate who we serve. We then have very specific products that we sell to them based on who they are. It's a flavor of a complete accounting and tax package based on the customer.

Embrace the idea of a product. As a CPA, we have been groomed to sell hours. Say goodbye to this mindset. We are now productizing a service. Products are the essential building blocks of any company. After all, it's the positive financial contribution and superior market performance of these products (and portfolios) that make the firm's long-term survival a competitive advantage. As a product manager, you are a guide who will ensure that your products are assets. You need to tend and nurture them so they produce a long-term financial return. Get a little lovey with your product. Does anyone in your firm today think and love the solution they sell? I believe CPAs care about their customers, but I don't believe they have an affection for their services. An hour is an hour is an hour. Imagine the culture that is created when you can love the productized services you create. Why is there love? One reason: You know in your heart that your solution matches their needs perfectly because it was created just for them. And they respond with equal love and referrals too!

Why is there love? One reason: You know in your heart that your solution matches their needs perfectly because it was created just for them. And they respond with equal love and referrals too!

Decide what it is you're selling. Whoever is creating products with technical tax or audit expertise will need to include a comprehensive understanding of the product's functionality and capability. The product manager must understand the customer's problem and needs and how the solution can solve that problem. This is where it it's so important to connect with the tax geek or audit master on your team. But, remember, the product manager does not need to have the deep technical expertise. That can be left to the subject matter expert.

> This also includes the technology used in the products you manage. Software systems, labor needs, processes, and communication components are included as well. How will your product be used by your customers? It also encompasses pricing models and marketing techniques as well as sales and distribution channels.
>
> The market in which your product is placed is equally important. You must know your domain and be able to demonstrate your knowledge and experience. Basically, you must know who you are selling to, where they frequent, and how the product's impact will affect your customer's life. You must walk the talk. You must know the many aspects of your targeted industry, such as its jargon, technology, and landscape—as well as other functions specifically related to your product. This can be broadly thought of as environmental domain. Where will the productized services be marketed and sold? Who is the right customer? What are the alternative products in the marketplace? You need to have this information and understand it well to be perceived as an industry expert. Hello, thought leadership!

The Persona: A Closer Look

At my firm, one of our big personas is a real estate investment firm. They like a one-stop shop. They like our personalized attention. They know that we have a certain amount of practical, specialized tax knowledge that they can use. What do they dislike? They dislike the detail, because they're deal guys, they're big picture guys, they just want to know: Can they defer the gain, can they not defer the gain, what is the gain? They tell us to take care of the details. Hands off, get it done yesterday, keep me out of jail, I hate taxes. I'm sure you know the type.

What are some of the challenges we have with them? They're hard to track down, they're somewhat disorganized, they're reactive, and there are deals flying all over. In fact, you probably have a real estate guy in your firm who looks just like this. We have several of them.

What's their responsibility? They need to provide us documentation, they need to keep us informed of any deal happening proactively, instead of sending us some closing statements and saying, "okay, I need to make an estimated payment on this." They may or may not be technical, but they're business savvy. They are often in their cars or on the golf course, and they live for sales. Knowing all this, we must think about how we're going to communicate with them. Yet, it's more than communication; it's also about data organization and data delivery for them. They live in a transaction-based world, which is very different than operating a small business. Who they are and how they do business impacts how we relate to them.

Let's look at another persona. One that I'm sure many of you experience: Joe Small Business. Mr. Business wants responsive action to their questions, they want a fair fee, they value what they're paying for, but they're concerned about price. They're not growing, so they feel like the same thing that happened this year is the same thing that happened last year. Their biggest goals are probably making sure they are complying and maintaining low taxes. They may or may not want advisory services, or they may or may not be willing to pay for advisory services. They want access to information. They may try to get away with everything. They sometimes even disagree with bank statements. I don't know if you have a client like that. They get caught up in immaterial issues sometimes, and they have multiple people with different agendas. Their skills are usually technical, but it's very specific to their field. Someone on their team usually has limited office knowledge. Usually there is an extra person between you and the business owner. Maybe they're that office manager, or the spouse who manages everything.

When you work with them, you're going to work with them very differently than when you work with your real estate guy. It's important to know who your customers are as you start to productize your service because that's going to help you figure out how you're going to serve them. And, of course, what you are going to sell them.

Another persona that we have is a graphic artist. They're the typical solopreneur. Usually, they're one or two people. They need handholding, they like simple software and minimum involvement, but they're pretty tech savvy. Sometimes they're flaky, they may get overwhelmed easily, they're not responsive, and their follow-up is sometimes terrible. We just let them do invoicing, and we do everything else on the back end. The way we interact with them is very different than how we interact with our Joe Small Business and very different than we act with our real estate guy.

What I'm trying to get at here is, as you start to productize your service, and you determine who you're serving from a practice management standpoint, it's going to help you to clarify how you're going to serve them, what you're going to sell them, and how you're going to sell it.

You're no longer going to be selling time for value because you're going to put something special into the bundle. This is going to help you.

If you can go back through your firm and figure out how you treat certain customers, and what's important to them, then you can help create products around that, and you can sell via fixed prices or value prices.

How to Create a Persona

Part of changing your business model is knowing whom you're going to serve.

To discover my firm's personas, we went through our customer list and grouped them into business-related and "What do they like?" categories.

Then we had a meeting and discussed the subsets and asked/responded to the below questions as a group.

We then documented the answers so our whole team would know and understand who we talk to daily.

It was funny that most of our customers fit into a subgrouping that we could define. We enjoyed the experience because it gave us new, organized information that helped us market our firm.

Aside from marketing, it's important to understand who you are communicating with and their point of view so that you can help them understand their solution.

The way we communicate is very different based on subgroups. If your whole team communicates to the right customer in the right way, the relationship stays with the solution, not with the partner.

When you are creating personas, start with these basic questions:
- What is your job role? Your job title?
- What is a typical day?
- What skills are required?
- What knowledge and tools do you use?
- Who do you report to? Who reports to you?

Goals
- What are you responsible for?

> - What does it mean to be successful in your role?
>
> **Challenges**
> - What are your biggest challenges?
> - How do you overcome these challenges?
>
> **Company**
> - What industry or industries does your company work in?
> - What is the size of your company (revenue, employees)?
>
> **Watering holes**
> - How do you learn about new information for your job?
> - What publications or blogs do you read?
> - What associations and social networks do you belong to?
>
> **Personal background**
> - Age
> - Family (single, partnered, children)
> - Education
>
> **Shopping preferences**
> - How to you prefer to interact with vendors (email, phone, in person)?
> - Do you use the Internet to research vendors or products? If yes, how do you search for information? What types of websites do you use?

And so, it would make sense that the next step is . . .

Create a product your customer loves. Seriously. What would make them do cartwheels and/or make their heart explode? I know it seems weird. But think about it: This concept allows for less dependency on relationships because they love the product, not the provider. This is how we must start thinking about what it is we sell. You must understand the customer's need. The customer doesn't know how their product should work or perform. They just know how they feel and what problem the solution solves. And therefore, they fall in love with the result. This is one of the biggest issues I see in CPA firms today. When you focus on selling time and billing, your focus is on yourself. But when you create productized services, your focus is on your customer.

When you focus on selling time and billing, your focus is on yourself. But when you create productized services, your focus is on your customer. Your customer should always come first.

Your customer should always come first. CPAs typically say that in their marketing materials and pitches, but it's not true.

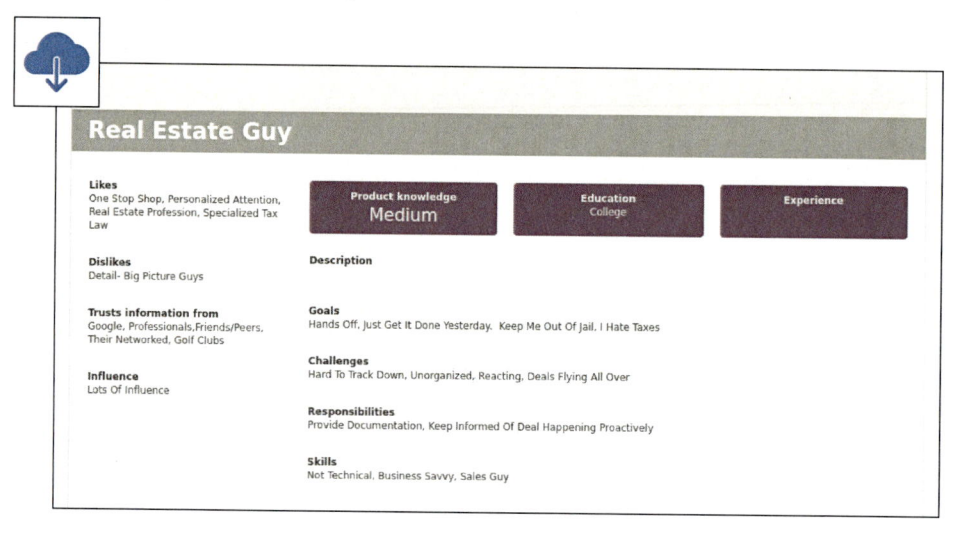

Real Estate Guy

Likes
One Stop Shop, Personalized Attention, Real Estate Profession, Specialized Tax Law

Dislikes
Detail- Big Picture Guys

Trusts information from
Google, Professionals, Friends/Peers, Their Networked, Golf Clubs

Influence
Lots Of Influence

Product knowledge: Medium
Education: College
Experience:

Description

Goals
Hands Off. Just Get It Done Yesterday. Keep Me Out Of Jail. I Hate Taxes

Challenges
Hard To Track Down, Unorganized, Reacting, Deals Flying All Over

Responsibilities
Provide Documentation, Keep Informed Of Deal Happening Proactively

Skills
Not Technical, Business Savvy, Sales Guy

Persona Template aha

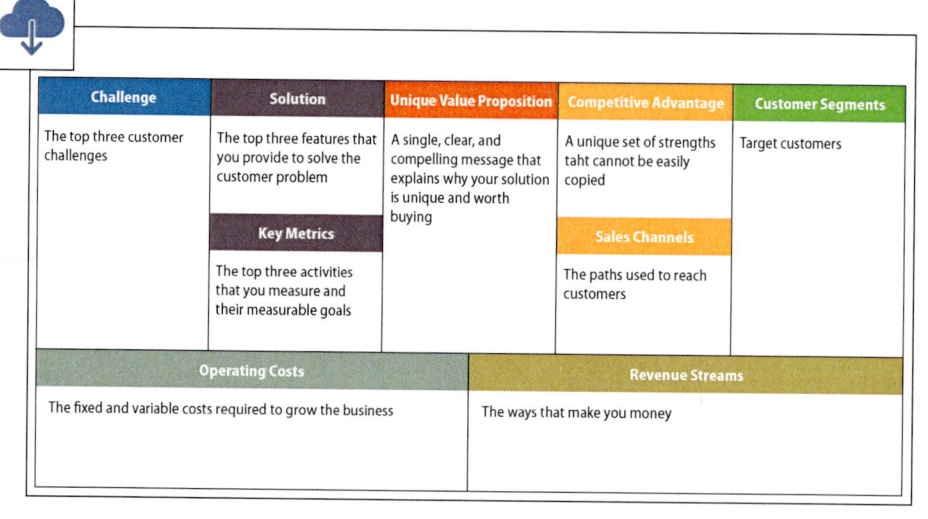

Challenge	Solution	Unique Value Proposition	Competitive Advantage	Customer Segments
The top three customer challenges	The top three features that you provide to solve the customer problem	A single, clear, and compelling message that explains why your solution is unique and worth buying	A unique set of strengths taht cannot be easily copied	Target customers
	Key Metrics		**Sales Channels**	
	The top three activities that you measure and their measurable goals		The paths used to reach customers	

Operating Costs	Revenue Streams
The fixed and variable costs required to grow the business	The ways that make you money

Business Model Template aha!

Goals, Goals, Goals

Now that we know who our customers are and our desired business model, we're going to think about what we're going to do for the rest of the year. We're going to create goals!

I've talked about Aha! and how that helps me set a course for my firm. But what I really like about the platform is that once you create goals, you can move them around. And it's not a big deal! Brand might be important to you today, but later it might be something else. You can set up your goals for the year using this technology, and then after you have your goals, you can add in initiatives to support them.

Too many firms don't meet their initiatives with their goals. Or the goals happen in the partner meeting, and then the initiatives fall off. By having them all tied together, you can have accountability. When you have your initiatives, goals, and strategic plan all in one place, on a platform that allows you to experiment and regularly make changes, then you can see what work is being done to serve your customers. It can be immensely helpful as a firm leader to have this at your fingertips.

The other thing I love about Aha! is that you can move around your priorities. How many of you still use lists on your desk? It can work sometimes, but what happens if they disappear? Are you able to easily prioritize them? I use this technology to keep track of my ever-changing priorities.

Ask tough questions that relate to your goals. What's your payroll process? Have you designed it? Are you going to have a ticket system? Do you have a new website? Are you putting together a mobile app? Are you going to use AutoFlow? You know, most of us have these questions floating around in our head. It doesn't have to be that way. You could put all those initiatives together, prioritize them, and then put timelines around them! Who's paying attention to timelines that are not deadline-related? Not many of us! CPAs are notorious for saying, "Oh, we're going to do it." Then somehow, it's tax season again and what we wanted to get accomplished didn't get done. Why? Because we don't have any way to follow through with our initiatives while keeping everybody on the same page, all moving the way we need to be moving.

The next-level Radical CPA knows this way of (not) doing is over.

It's no longer, "Oh, I can wait until next year to do this." Now you have a place to start—and it's the roadmap. It gives you a place to put your to-dos and your details, so if you wanted to move towards customer selection or pricing, you could put your goals around it.

So, you have assessed your firm's skill set, developed a roadmap, and identified your main customer personas, and you are starting to build your products around your customers' needs and wants. Now what else should you be thinking about? Believe me when I say, there's always something!

Build strong teams. How do you a build a team? What does it take? How does personality and skillset get considered, especially when you're going up against the old-school mentality that was built in a service of hours business? There is going to be a lot of change happening. Be prepared for lots of questioning and ridicule from old-school partners. Think ahead about engaging those naysayers. Keep your enemies close. Do you want to put that difficult partner on the project so you can control the conversation? To be successful, you must be savvy in networking, in office politics, and in influencing. You must let your insides come out. You must show people who you are—your strengths, weaknesses, likes, dislikes. And you need passion. Show it. Live it. Breathe it.

Master your processes. I can't say this enough. In fact, I'll say it again: Master your processes. I knew I was onto something in the chapter on process and design thinking in my last book. But it's now gone beyond those concepts. Within the context of product management, process becomes a powerhouse to your firm. Efficient and effective processes are what will make your firm's product profitable and scalable. The ability to iterate on your process over time allows for constant improvement.

Know your data. Data matters. We all know this. We love our numbers and our graphs and our calculations. Data is like a gold in an organization. For both you and your customers. Be open to where new data will come from. A timesheet is not the right data point. Is data from your workflow software the correct data point to determine capacity? How long do items sit in your firm? How much work can you do before you need to add additional headcount? Is it quantifiable by number of customers or gross billings? How will your team leverage customer service? These are all things never given to us via a timesheet. And how quickly do returns get out of your door? Workflow needs to be one of your new measurements for productivity. How fast projects are moving through your firm is important. Possibly. What about emojis for customer service? Have you given your customers a survey for benchmarking? A popular survey is the NPS or Net Promoter Score. You might get a lot of information from a survey. Be open to all types of data, both concrete and subjective.

Decide to platformize or productize. In the above paragraphs, I detailed why firms should productize their services instead of sell hours. A unique business model that is also potentially transformative to your business is the platformization of firm services. One firm doing just this is Accodex from Australia. The idea is that the process becomes a platform to deliver services. Is one business model better than the other? Both lead us into the future.

Take for example, Feng Zhu and Nathan Furr's 2016 Harvard Business Review article, "Products to Platforms: Making the Leap." The authors write: "In a product business model, firms create value by developing differentiated products for specific customer needs, and they capture value by charging money for those items. In a platform business model, firms create value primarily by connecting users and third parties, and they capture value by charging fees for access to the platform. Platform models bring a shift in emphasis—from meeting specific customer needs to encourage mass-market adoption to maximize the number of interactions, or from product-related sources of competitive advantage (such as product differentiation) to network-related sources of competitive advantage (the network effects of connecting many users and third parties)."

A Platform for Practice Management:
An Interview With Chris Hooper of Accodex

By Kayleigh Padar

Chris Hooper, the CEO and managing partner of Accodex, recently redesigned the firm's business model to respond to clients' changing accounting needs. The firm operates in four areas: the United States, the United Kingdom, Australia, and the Philippines. It is made up of over 50 employees.

"I started with a small practice in 2011 in Australia," Hooper said. "It was 100 percent cloud, fixed fee, global from the get-go. There wasn't really a need to change those fundamentals."

The fact that the firm was already technologically advanced meant that further change was a little easier to accomplish.

"There wasn't really a culture shift; it was hard-wired into our DNA from the get-go. To perpetuate it though, I think vision is the most important value," Hooper said.

Despite beginning with a firm that seemed sufficiently modernized, more change needed to occur in the business model area, rather than with the technology.

"Instead of running a traditional partnership or corporate structure, we separated the operations from the practice, essentially creating a platform. This allows us to admit new partners without bottlenecks," Hooper said.

To make this model possible, the firm created its own online platform that includes CRM, workflow management, client portals, and enterprise communications. "This was essential for us to deliver on the platform business model," Hooper said.

Almost the entire company operates remotely, without most employees needing to come to a specific office building.

"Remote work is essential to scaling globally. That being said, I still believe centralized operations need to be based in a real office. I think it speeds up collaboration," Hooper said.

Customer prices are based on the value of their work, although some projects are billed by the hour when the scope is impossible to define.

Although some prospective clients aren't always comfortable with the cloud technology, the firm simply refers them to other companies that are more able to suit their needs. Despite these few prospective clients, the firm's revenue has consistently grown at a 10 - 20 percent increase per month.

"The awards and accolades we've received to date are what I'm most proud of. It is nice to get external confirmation that you're on the bleeding edge," Hooper said.

Happy Tax: Why You Need to Know Their Name

What if tax CPAs charged labor for a platform and were not even a firm, but part of a franchise and technology play?

This is the story of Happy Tax. And they are changing the nature of our business as we know it.

Happy Tax is a franchise model. In this case, the franchisees are the business development and sales arm, and tax CPAs stay behind the platform working in a "gig economy" role. It just so happens that CPAs log into preparing tax returns just as an Uber driver shows up to drive.

The company grew by 300 percent in 2016 alone.

Happy Tax launched in April of 2015 to solve the broken problem of retail tax prep. They are capitalizing on the gig economy and utilizing a labor pool of side jobs, retired CPAs, and those who are in-between. Be it franchisees or CPAs who want something different.

They have isolated the roles of the positions to allow the sales/customer service people to do what they do best and the technical CPAs do what they do best. A successful serial entrepreneur, Mario Costanz, who is the CEO of Happy Tax, built and sold 99 tax prep franchises, and is now ready to disrupt the retail tax prep market.

CHAPTER 4
Embrace Difference & Diversity

By Liz Gold

Difference comes in many forms. Race, gender identity, sexual orientation, religion, age, ability, learning style, personality—these characteristics are only just a few of the many that make us who we are, yet isn't it amazing that many of us only bring a fraction of ourselves to work?

Diversity is a loaded word. August de los Reyes is the head of design and research at Pinterest. In a TechCrunch video, he talks about the connotative baggage that comes along with the term "diversity," preferring to take the term in the literal sense.

"Diversity is about a spectrum of thoughts, experiences, approaches, and it's actually a great thing for design," he said. "[In] product development today, it's just understood that there's diversity of expertise. We have people for multiple functions, design, engineering, program management, marketing—that is diversity right there, and no one questions it. It requires different sets of expertise to produce a great experience. Well, what happens is, if we look at other pivots of diversity, particularly with design, it actually opens up more opportunities for innovation for better outcomes."

The same point can be related to accounting. A successful firm is a sum of its many parts. There's the partnership, the service lines, the industries, the employees, IT, marketing, business development, facilities, you get the idea. It's expected that each of these departments brings their own skills and expertise to the table to keep the firm sustainable and growing.

Innovation will happen when we let go of how things have always been done and are open to different ways of doing things and different types of people doing those things. So, when we pivot, like de los Reyes says, to consider a different type of diversity, we expand and prepare better for our outcome—whatever that might be—and create a much more inclusive experience.

Cultural Intelligence = Innovation

We all know the working world has gone global. Small businesses can compete with the big, and the cloud has transformed the way people sell, market, and conduct transactions. So, it makes sense that the more aware we are about other cultures and geographies and people, the better our business relationships will be.

A good place to start is with cultural intelligence. According to Rhodes Perry of Rhodes Perry Consulting, a global strategic management firm helping executives build LGBTQ+ diverse and inclusive workplace cultures, there are two spectrums in a workplace: one of similarities, where employees are working towards a shared goal with general group buy-in, and the other of differences, which includes people with various identities, experiences, ideas, and various ways of being.

When a company is aligned with its cultural intelligence, they are leveraging those differences to move towards that shared goal. "It's somewhat simple," said Perry. "We need to have different perspectives to generate new ideas, get out of group-think, which can inspire people to share their ideas, become more engaged and productive, and that's where the sweet spot of innovation comes in."

Not only that, Perry said, but when an employer invests, understands, and affirms those differences, they are going to be more likely to attract diverse talent—especially the younger generation, which highly values diversity among their peers—and a company who is going to celebrate who they are.

This is where top-level buy-in is critical.

"While putting policies in place that promote diversity and inclusion is certainly a step in the right direction, leaders should be committed to making sure that they are being followed," said Kimberly Ellison-Taylor, CPA CGMA, and global accounting strategy director for the financial and professional services industries for Oracle America. "I've found that if the tone at the top is followed up with a real commitment by holding all leaders accountable to an inclusive workplace, it resonates with the employees."

From The Trenches

Here are a few statistics from the website Diversity Best Practices, a division of Working Mother Media, regarding a population that exists in accounting firms (and well, in all workplaces) but is rarely addressed:
- Over half of LGBT employees hide their sexual orientation at work.
- One in four LGBT employees report hearing derogatory jokes or negative comments such as "that's so gay" while at work.
- A fifth of LGBT workers report looking for a job specifically because the environment at the current job isn't accepting of LGBT identities.

It's real. I know, because I've experienced it.

Many corporate environments have teeth; that is, they can be harsh for creative people, demoralizing for sensitive people, and alienating for anyone who doesn't fit into the dominant culture. Like many of us, I've had a long history of not being able to fit in even though I would try profusely. I never truly felt like I could really own my identity as a queer woman when I worked in corporate environments. Some workplaces were better than others, but my experience has made a lasting impression and given me a strong distaste of working inside large companies. Plainly said, it's been hard to find my people.

You might not want to hear this. But, I've had male colleagues and yes, supervisors and company leaders, make disparaging sexist and transphobic comments degrading women in front of me at formal meetings, where I was the only woman.

I've had a male boss stand behind me, directing me to watch a YouTube video of men talking about female genitalia, while another male boss sat across from me and laughed.

I've had a female coworker make jokes about Jewish people in front of three or four team members, even though we were working at a Jewish-owned company (I did end up talking with her privately about it, which was one of the hardest things I've ever done.)

And I can't tell you how many homophobic comments I've heard over the course of my years. Sexism, racism, homophobia, transphobia, ageism and a whole host of other oppressive language, actions, and behaviors run rampant in companies. No HR video will stop it, and as firm owners, you must take responsibility.

Have these experiences left me with a bad taste in my mouth? Yes. But did I learn something from it? Of course.

Many people might say, well, why didn't you speak up? Why didn't you say something?

There were instances I did—to the best of my ability. But the reality was, I didn't want to be different, I didn't want to start something. I didn't want people to make fun of me, I didn't want people to talk about me behind my back, or worse, stop talking when I approached. I wanted to fit in. I wanted to be a team player. Not speaking up and interrupting: That is what dominant culture dictates. And team culture, unfortunately, can be cruel.

I'm here to tell you, my story is not unique. This is a big reason why bright, creative people walk out your door. And this is one of the underlying reasons why many young people are leaving the accounting profession. Who wants to commit their time and energy to a firm or company where they can't be themselves? Where they don't see others like them among the leadership ranks? Where, when they do get through the doors, there is no one they can truly relate to and very little, if any, support for how to build relationships with their colleagues and managers? How long are people (let's face it, Millennials and Generation Z employees) willing to stay at a firm or in a workplace that doesn't acknowledge different identities? That assumes everyone is straight, or white, or able-bodied, or productive in the same way? Not long.

We're living in a global society. Millennials don't even blink at multiculturalism, but they do notice it when it's not present in the room.

A Legacy of Leadership

Though it is slowly changing, most accounting firms are traditional in the sense that they are still owned and managed by white, Baby Boomer-aged men wearing nice suits and ties. It's been the go-to standard for decades. Slowly, I would argue, more hoodies and hip sneakers are taking over the suits, as is common in startup culture, but this obviously depends on the firm and its customers.

And while technology may be changing at the speed of light, firm processes are getting more streamlined, and even more firms are looking to value pricing because they just understand the limitations of timesheets, change also needs to be happening from a talent and business development perspective.

A diverse staff leads to diverse clients.

A more diverse client base results in more challenging work, higher profits, and long-term growth.

Recognizing and making decisions upon this connection can help tackle the seemingly insurmountable challenge of succession planning as well as the staffing shortage that just seems to get worse.

But first, let me say this. Accounting firm veterans, the profession's legacy partners (a majority of whom are older white men) come with historical, institutional knowledge that cannot be replaced or duplicated. They've lived through decades upon decades of change, and many have made it through the ups and downs successfully. Many have compelling stories and insight to share.

Talking about diversity and difference and inclusion does not erase that.

After all, they've built great and memorable companies and shared what they know (even if the feedback is hard to hear, they often have good points); many of them have helped countless people grow and prosper at all stages in their careers, and have served as excellent mentors to people of all ages and genders.

But they, like all of us, are not without their biases and blind spots. And many aren't even aware of them. How could they be? It's hard to know what we are not familiar with or don't understand—especially if it's never been on our radar before. And when you've been living large in a boys' club, let's be real, you can feel resistant to letting others in.

We need legacy partners to come forward and fight the good fight. In fact, while there is a grace in knowing when to retire, like Jen Wilson of Convergence Coaching said, the other side of that is, if the old guys aren't ready to go, train them in the new ways!

"Baby Boomers are not ready to retire," said Tamika Cody, former managing editor of *Accounting Today*. "They are saying, 'I want to do more and my organization pushed me out. I want to stay and consult.' The industry heads aren't going to train the old guys, so offer the necessary technology training, and let them tell you they don't need anything else."

I agree. Put the old guys to work.

However, with the caveat that the world is changing. And the legacy leaders in the accounting world must change, too. Where to start? Consider the following:

- Check your influence. Take stock of how much space you take up in a meeting, how your energy shifts the dynamics of a room, how people's engagement changes when you are "just sitting in on" a meeting.
- Share your power. You have a lot of it. And your decision-making impacts other people. Delegate what you can. Empower others to take ownership. Give others prime opportunities.
- Watch the jokes. Language and how we talk to each other in the workplace has changed. Not only because it's "politically correct," but because you want to be respectful and you don't always know who's in the room listening.
- Acknowledge that your intention might not always match your impact. And people might not always want your help or input.
- Be ready to be challenged on your ideas.
- Be generous with your time and expertise: Ask your employees where they want to go with their careers and how you can help get them there.
- Know when it's time to let go of something you've been doing for like, forever. Pass it on. Teach it to someone new and watch them make it their own.
- Listen and ask questions! Really hear what people are telling you (and be aware of what they are not telling you). Be OK with not knowing all the latest of everything. Humility goes a long way.

Makes sense, right?

What I'm talking about—and what the Radical CPA brand is all about—is that the traditional accounting firm culture comprises a social capital and political system that needs to transform, making room for others to emerge, innovate, and lead. Some people will need to move over, some people need to pull more people up, but one things for sure: Opportunity needs to be available to everyone, and there must be a new culture of respect where people learn from each other. Acceptance of difference needs to be part of the equation. And for all of this to be truly successful (and, frankly, less painful), we need our legacy partners to be champions in this cause.

Breaking It Down

More than a decade ago, when I first joined the editorial team at Accounting Today, and started working the beat, I didn't know what to expect. But I quickly realized that despite the profession being conservative, and finding the homogeneousness of managing partners stifling, I was seeing this undercurrent of women and people of color (POC) and young people emerging. At least, I was looking for them. I knew it then and I know it now: This new demographic with a passion for accounting as the common denominator would be the future.

And it is.

However, I can't speak for everyone. I can just tell you what I've seen and what I've experienced. I have my own blind spots. And the truth is, people of color might beg to differ.

According to Cody, many people of color don't see others like them in mid-sized accounting firms; many still get overlooked for jobs even though they have all the top-notch qualifications and skills and outstanding resumes.

Is that happening in your firm?

When you talk about diversity and inclusion, you must break it down. You may say you have diversity in your firm, but what population is diverse?

According to Perry, "It's likely that your frontline staff, or your entry level staff positions are where you have the most diversity." But as Perry pointed out and what rings true in many accounting firms, as you travel up the hierarchy, it becomes more reflective of the dominant Baby Boomer culture—and in most instances, it means whiter and more male the higher you go.

Perry added that inclusion happens when you stitch employees into the most important parts of the organization—in leadership positions—and you are actively engaging them through committee responsibilities, where they can share their ideas and use them for strategic decision-making. This leads to innovation and higher levels of performance . . . not to mention an increase in the bottom line.

But why is being intentional about this important?

Let's look at some stats. Eighty-five percent of professional staff at CPA firms are white, according to the AICPA's 2015 report, "Trends in the Supply of Accounting Graduates and the Demand for Public Accounting Recruits." The same survey reports that 31 percent of new hires in 2013 - 2014 were women of color. Half of people of color do not feel obliged to stay at their current firm, according to the U.S. Equal Employment Opportunity Commission's 2014 National Aggregate Report of Accounting, Tax Preparation, Bookkeeping, and Payroll Services, *"Job Patterns for Minorities and Women in Private Industry."* According to the 2015 Accounting MOVE Project Report, women are 47 percent of all professional staff at CPA firms, but make up just 22 percent of partners and principals. It is getting better, albeit slowly: The percentage of women on management committees is growing, to 23 percent in 2015, up from 17 percent in 2011.

The AICPA is working on improving those numbers. They posted a statement articulating the business case for diversity and inclusion on their website, and they introduced their National Commission on Diversity & Inclusion in September 2012.

"One of the focuses of the group has been shifting the understanding of why diversity and inclusion is important," said Ellison-Taylor. "It's more than the right thing to do; it's a business imperative with the shifts in the U.S. demographics and rise in entrepreneurial capital among minorities. As the business case continues to crystalize and become more of a reality around the country, the conversation around diversity and inclusion shifts from 'why' to 'how.'"

Ellison-Taylor, who is the first female African-American chairman of AICPA's board of directors, pointed to several resources from the AICPA that can help this endeavor. There's the Accounting Inclusion Maturity Model, a tool designed to help firms determine where they are in their efforts and what it would take to get them to where they want to be. There's a recruitment and retention toolkit that provides firms with step-by-step actions on attracting, recruiting, and retaining diverse talent, while addressing topics such as creating a culture of inclusion and unconscious bias.

"If a firm would like to engage a more diverse workforce, they need to show up where they grow up, meaning they should ensure their leaders and their company brand are familiar to diverse talent," Ellison-Taylor said. "This can be achieved by spending quality time on campuses, clubs, and organizations where diverse talent is being groomed for the profession."

Create Equity

So, we know you can't just put the diversity and inclusion phrase on marketing materials and call it good. There needs to be some substance behind the claim. And part of that substance includes looking at the word "equity" and considering how you can provide equitable opportunities and growth potential to every individual in your firm.

Remember, this is not about special privileges, said Perry. "This is about creating workplace equity, or guaranteed fair treatment, access, opportunity, and advancement for all employees, while simultaneously striving to identify and eliminate barriers that have prevented the full participation of underrepresented groups in a workplace." How do you do this, especially if you want to make it to the Top 200?

- **Look around.** Take a real hard look at your employee numbers. What are your demographics? How many people of color do you have in your firm? What are their roles? And what groups are represented? If you have 175 partners in your firm and you can count the people of color on one hand—that's too small of a number to call yourself diverse. What about people with disabilities? Or LGBT people? Or veterans and retirees?

- **Get to know your people.** It may seem obvious, but you'd be surprised at the number of companies that really don't know their employees. Find out their values, their passions, their skill sets, what's important to them, what their particular needs are around balancing work and life. And find out what success means to them, so you can create a roadmap to help them get there.

- **Bypass assumptions.** You may think you know someone because of their skin color or last name or religious beliefs, or because they told you they have a same-sex partner. That does not mean you know them! Create space for people to be individuals, and respect their right to share information with you as they feel comfortable. And, be aware they always have a choice to not share anything at all. Some people are private and choose not to bring everything to their place of work.

- **Be aware.** Talking about diversity—especially race—can be very difficult, and many companies prefer to gloss over these conversations. But the reality is, to be inclusive is to be able to include everyone. Be aware of your blind spots, and know that despite some of your best intentions you might leave someone out. Or someone will inadvertently be left off a calendar invite for a meeting. Or you'll be talking about diversity without an LGBT individual or person of color in the room. Take notice of who is in attendance and participating.

- **Understand the importance of representation, not tokenism.** Look at your website and marketing materials. Are they modern and relevant? Are they truly representative of your firm? It's common knowledge that a website is an extension of your business. If you have a mediocre website, that is going to send an impression. "Visuals can turn off top talent, especially younger professionals, who are more likely to evaluate a company based on its digital footprint," said Perry. "If I don't see myself in those pictures, or if I don't see a diversity vision with a plan that demonstrates action on the vision, I don't see myself fitting in there."

It's important to add, however, you don't want to tokenize a person of color or another minority in the process. This means, don't recruit a small number of people (or one person) from underrepresented groups to give the appearance of diversity within your firm. In accounting firms, it's a challenge to bypass tokenism. The answer? Hire more people of color and create a culture of inclusiveness from the get-go. Make sure you have POC in leadership. Ask yourself, how can I make sure people are represented here, not tokenized? It starts with awareness and working with someone to build out a diversity and inclusion initiative.

It's very easy to gravitate towards people who look like you and walk similarly in the world. This is what we call unconscious bias. In the AICPA's Recruitment and Retention Toolkit: A Journey Toward a More Inclusive Workforce, unconscious bias is defined as our natural people preferences. "Biologically we are hardwired to prefer people who look like us, sound like us, and share our interests," the report says. "When looking to increase the number of diverse hires within your organization, a critical first step is to address unconscious bias across the organization, helping management and staff understand the importance of diversity awareness, and communicating about and managing constructive conflict."

The bottom line is that without equity, diversity and inclusion are merely good intentions. But there's something missing: action.

In the *Inside Higher Ed* article "Language of Appeasement," Dr. Dafina-Lazarus Stewart wrote, "Diversity asks, 'Who's in the room?' Equity responds: 'Who is trying to get in the room but can't?' Whose presence in the room is under constant threat of erasure?" And while this article is obviously addressed at academia, the sentiment remains: Let's go beyond the rhetoric and start asking the tough questions about who is really thriving in accounting firms today.

Ellison-Taylor maintains a glass-half-full perspective as it relates to her career at the intersection of accounting and technology. "I grew up with parents who were very clear to remind me that I can't change anyone else or what they do, but that I can control how I respond," she said. "Using that backdrop, I always studied my colleagues and leaders to analyze their path, their work approaches, strengths, network, etc., and then would do a SWOT against my own various areas. This assessment over the years has informed my personal philosophy on leadership and success."

That philosophy includes positive attitude, hard work, strong work ethic, persistence, confidence, stepping out of her comfort zone, team building, negotiation, and a commitment to life-long learning. All these attributes are core components as to how Ellison-Taylor engages with her colleagues in accounting and technology. "There will always be areas that need improvement, and there will always be individuals across every industry who are not comfortable with differences—yet when faced with where to expend my energy, I would much rather focus on what I learned as a little girl: Change what you can and demonstrate through your actions the winning path," she said.

Creating More Diversity in Accounting Firm Leadership:
A Q&A with Donny Shimamoto, CPA, CITP, CGMA, and Managing Director of IntrapriseTechKnowlogies LLC

Liz Gold: Do you think the profession is getting better in terms of more people of color in leadership positions? Why or why not?

DS: The profession is getting a little better, but there is a distinct lack of Asian-American professionals in leadership positions in the AICPA volunteer ranks. Over three years ago, when I was chair of the AICPA's Information Technology and Technology Assurance Executive Committee, I was invited to attend an all-chairs meeting in the AICPA's NYC offices. All of the committee chairs were older white men, and there was one older white female and me—only two of us representing "diversity" and only myself being non-white. And even though Asian Americans compose the second largest population of accountants and auditors in the US—yes, more than African- and Hispanic-Americans—there is still a distinct lack of Asian-Americans representation in key volunteer leadership positions in the AICPA.

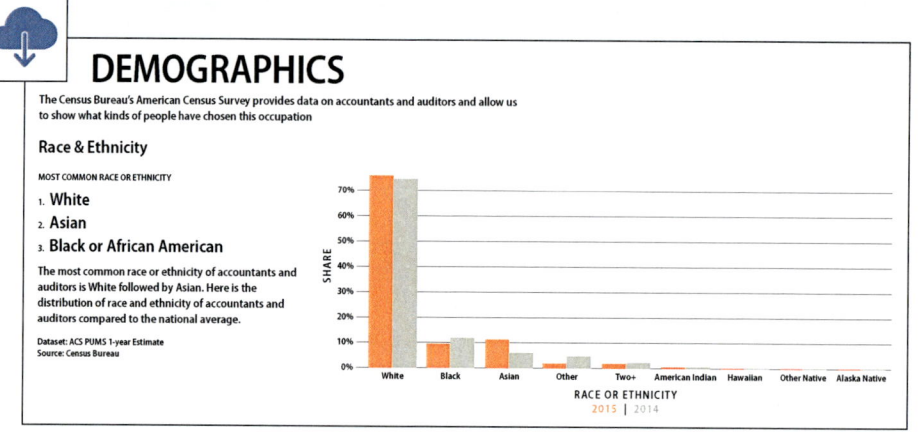

DEMOGRAPHICS

The Census Bureau's American Census Survey provides data on accountants and auditors and allow us to show what kinds of people have chosen this occupation

Race & Ethnicity

MOST COMMON RACE OR ETHNICITY
1. White
2. Asian
3. Black or African American

The most common race or ethnicity of accountants and auditors is White followed by Asian. Here is the distribution of race and ethnicity of accountants and auditors compared to the national average.

Dataset: ACS PUMS 1-year Estimate
Source: Census Bureau

Census Bureau's report on racial and ethnic breakdown within the accounting/auditing professions

LG: What are the barriers that you see preventing people of color from being in leadership positions within firms and within their associations?

DS: I think the biggest barrier is the white male and "country club" culture that underlies many of the firms' and associations' leadership groups. When I would sit at the dinners and socialize with the other white male leaders in the profession, when not about accounting, the conversation was often about either sports, boating, golf, or other topics associated with the "upper crust" of society. As someone coming from a lower middle class family and Asian ethnic background, these were things that I couldn't relate to—only rich and white people did that kind of stuff—and it made me feel distinctly out of place and not want to be there.

LG: **Have you experienced any outward racism (or micro-aggressions) that you would be willing to share?**

DS: I haven't experienced any direct racism—I think people in the profession are too aware of the possibility of being perceived as racist to behave in that way—but I have felt like I've been discounted as an Asian-American. I had one email exchange with a senior AICPA executive where the person insisted that there is diversity in the leadership of the profession, citing African-American and Hispanic-American members of the board. When I cited my experience at the chairs' meeting mentioned earlier and the lack of Asian-American representation in the committee chairs' positions or at board level, the person continued to emphasize that there was diversity. This really made me feel like Asian-Americans simply don't matter in the eyes of the AICPA.

LG: **What advice do you have for 1) firms for bringing more people of color into leadership roles and 2) for the profession as a whole to step it up?**

DS: If white male-dominated firms want more people of color to feel welcome in leadership roles, I think they need to look at the underlying social norms and relationships that they operate under, and ensure that it is something that doesn't put the person of color into an uncomfortable situation. So, don't invite me to come to the country club (where everyone else except me will be white) and golf (I don't golf) to get to know me better. I'd much rather have a nice dinner together. Also, don't make assumptions based on ethnic generalizations. For example, since my last name is Japanese, people automatically assume I like sushi. I don't not like sushi, but I'd much rather have a juicy pork chop or a tasty salad than sushi.

The profession as a whole is doing a lot to help raise the awareness of the need for diversity, but I feel like it's very similar to past Affirmative Action initiatives. My main concern with Affirmative Action is how it actually created situations of reverse discrimination for white people and later for Asian-American people, particularly in areas where there were high Asian-American populations, like California. Instead I think it is important to identify high potential people of color and to provide them with opportunities to be role models, and to help make them visible so that younger people of color in the profession have someone that they can relate to in the upper leadership ranks that makes them feel like there is opportunity and a place for them in the profession.

How diverse is your client base?

We've been talking a lot about why it's important to have diversity and difference at your firm on all levels. Diversity, inclusion, and equity are a power team that you need present at every table—it will bring new energy, conflict, disruption, stellar ideas, and innovation, and make your firm extremely marketable—not to mention profitable. The more diverse you are, the more relevant you are.

Having a diverse team leads to landing diverse clients. Who doesn't want a diverse client base in every sense of the word? It will help you attract more people, people who are outside your usual target clients, but who need and want your services and expertise because what you are doing resonates with them.

For instance, do you have any same-sex couples on your client list? Working with same-sex or LGBT couples who are unmarried can be profitable for your firm due to the complexities in tax and estate planning. Think about it: More challenges mean more consulting time and a more complex return. Success with that couple likely means referrals, and before you know it, you are building out a new niche in your firm.

Consider these statistics regarding buying power in Diversity Best Practices: Almost one in four LGBT adults in one year switched to a product or service because the new company supported the LGBT community, and 71 percent of lesbian and gay people remain loyal to a brand that is sympathetic to

LGBT issues even if the brand is costlier or less convenient.

"Groom your clients for diversity and inclusion," said Cody. "You have to look at your clients and see if they are diverse. If not, start looking for diverse clients. It's up to the partners to include the women, the people of color, the LGBT individuals. Make introductions."

Big or small, have the courage to create your culture…consciously

There's a lot of talk about accountability and transparency in both old-school firms and New Firms. People love to bounce those buzzwords around—but the truth is, being truly accountable and transparent takes courage. Whether you are a well-established firm looking to enhance your culture or a startup wanting to be strategic before you head to market, I would hope these two elements would be foundational to your firm values.

Think about what sort of firm you are and where you want to be. Think about who you are serving and how you are serving them. Think about the technology you choose and use. Think about how you communicate to your customers, prospects, and employees. And think about the people who you are grooming or choosing to be leaders—who are they, and can you genuinely say it's a diverse group?

Embracing difference will grow your firm. You will get more business, your team will be better for it, and you will come up with more innovative solutions to your customers' most pressing questions.

More gaps will close and more doors will open. And who doesn't want that?

Liz Gold has been writing about the accounting profession for over a decade. Her specialty areas include radical people, ideas and progressive social change. A former senior editor at Accounting Today, she is the founder and CEO of Rhino Girl Media, a media company that helps accounting firms, companies and individuals evolve their brand voice and advance their mission.

5 Ways to Create a More Diverse and Inclusive Workplace

By Minda Harts

When you think about the structural elements it will take to create a company culture that is both diverse and inclusive, what comes to mind?

Real cultural shifts take time, money, and buy-in from all stakeholders. A more diverse and inclusive environment is not only intended for internal use, but will also help you attract and retain more diverse clientele. Verna Myers said it best: "Diversity is being invited to the party, inclusion is being asked to dance."

Companies can no longer view their diversity and inclusion initiatives as "meets expectations." Companies must take a hard look and consider the proper strategies that will take their business from checking the box to being a champion in the accounting industry for diversity and inclusion. Many companies pat themselves on the back when they employ less than five percent women and underrepresented groups, and increase it the following year by a percentage point.

One could say they did, in fact, make progress, but that's what I consider passive progress, not intentional progress.

As a woman of color, I spent two decades working in environments that were not diverse and minimally inclusive. As someone who has experienced diversity and inclusion initiatives that were well-intentioned, yet that over time eventually fell short, my hope is that you find ways to implement or enhance your D&I initiatives. Have structured meetings with your senior leadership on how they can play an active role in shifting the culture.

Consider implementing these five steps to create a company culture that is both diverse and inclusive. These steps will help you access your company's current culture and foster future change.

1. Passive Versus Intentional Initiatives

Hiring a D&I director is a great first step. If your firm does not have someone overseeing your diversity and inclusion department, or you do not have one, this is your first benchmark.

Creating this department or having someone designated to support your diverse talent sends a strong signal that diversity and inclusion are important to your firm. Your company is being intentional in creating an environment where all employees can thrive and have an equal playing field.

Being diverse is not only race-related, but includes gender, religion, and sexual orientation to name a few other categories. We often think that diversity means only race, yet having an inclusive environment spans much further. Perhaps your current workforce is not inclusive, but now provides an opportunity to prepare for future employees and the environment you want them to experience on day one.

I remember consulting with a D&I director of a Fortune 500 company who oversaw an affinity group of color. Oddly enough, the woman managing this group was Caucasian. It was hard for me to believe that there was no one qualified to oversee an affinity group of color who is also someone of color. In this example, you are sending another wrong signal: 1) You realize the need to have an affinity group of color, but 2) You hire someone who doesn't adequately represent the group, and 3) You did not take the time to hire someone who would be their best advocate. Does this mean no one of color is qualified for this role? My guess is this was not the company's intent, but this is a strong case of passive progress.

When senior leaders take on this type of mindset, they are not doing their diverse talent any favors; they are reaffirming that diversity and inclusion are not a priority. A more intentional approach would be to hire someone who represents that particular affinity group to speak on their behalf. Someone in the company this population can identify with. It is crucial for businesses to understand that while diversity matters, representation matters even more.

When you think about the culture you want to create, ask the following question: Are we just checking a box or are we signaling to the rest of the company we are taking deliberate steps to create a culture with a winning strategy? Do not settle for receiving a passing grade. If you already have someone overseeing this department, ask yourself: Is this the right person to represent this group? Are they actively engaging with our underrepresented groups and are their voices heard? Again, don't fall into the trap of assuming what your diverse talent needs.

Ask them!

Engagement is the best policy. Just because a Big Four firm has a program that functions in one manner doesn't mean that this is how you should run your diversity and inclusion initiatives. Find out what your employees need from you to be successful. The recipe to success is 360 engagement. This responsibility not only falls to your designated D&I director but additionally to your senior leadership—make sure they are engaged with your diverse talent as well. Having buy-in from decision makers is equally important. This culture should trickle down from the CEO to the secretary. All employees should view diversity and inclusion as part of the company's mission. Perhaps you are not in a position to create a robust plan; if so, I would suggest outsourcing to a firm that specializes in helping companies reach their maximum potential. At my company, The Memo LLC, one of our traditional services is conducting workshops for senior leaders on how to engage, retain, and manage diverse talent. All leaders/managers should understand the fundamentals of engaging diverse talent. If they have not been equipped with the skills to do so, or have never managed a team of diverse talent, you are going to run up against a lot of human resources related problems, which can lead to unconscious bias. It is beneficial that your leaders understand their role in creating a more diverse and inclusive work environment. You might also want to keep in mind that there are companies being graded on their diversity and you don't want yours to fall short.

2. Recruiting and Retaining Diverse Talent

In recent years, most of the publicity around diversity and inclusion has focused on recruiting diverse talent, yet this has sometimes left tenured employees feeling left out.

What are you doing for your talent once you hire them?

Employees already have a vested interest in seeing your business win, and should be retained accordingly. Some of these employees might be great candidates for leading an affinity group or getting promoted into your new Diversity and Inclusion director role. Create opportunities for your diverse talent!

The key to a sustainable diversity and inclusion plan requires all seats at the table taking a vested interest, from the top down. I would also suggest diversifying where you recruit your talent. Always drawing from the same talent pool is not a good sign of diversity or inclusion. Think outside the box. If you need more ideas on how, outsourcing to firms that specialize in recruiting and retaining diverse talent can help.

Let's say that you lack a diverse workforce concerning race. If you're looking to increase your percentage of black and brown employees, you might want to consider adding new schools to your recruiting calendar. Some historically black colleges and universities (HBCUs) have incredible talent getting ready to enter the workforce. Add one of these institutions that specializes in your industry and make the investment. Another solution is reaching out to the National Association of Black Accountants, an essential partnership that could help increase your pipeline and visibility. Thinking about ways to diversify your workforce is important. Consider offering flexible or telecommute options for mothers and fathers returning to work after parental leave (if your firm has parental leave). This will require your firm to be flexible and inclusive.

3. A Clear Path Toward the C-Suite

This brings me to my third point. Once you have been thoughtful and intentional about having a successful diversity and inclusion department, what is the career track for these individuals?

Historically, the accounting field has struggled with proper representation of minorities and women; as a consultant, I can tell you that this is one of the major areas in which employers fail. They have implemented D&I initiatives, meaning they are hiring more diverse talent, but then not promoting that talent, or hiring that talent into executive positions. It's not enough to say you hire diverse talent. Are you developing diverse talent?

If the answer is no, then how successful are your D&I initiatives?

This goes back to passive versus intentional. The goal should be, when you look around your leadership table, you see a slice of everyone in your company represented in some way, shape, or form. You can start with speakers at industry conferences. Are the speakers diverse? Women make up 57 percent of the workforce and ideally should represent the same percentage in senior roles and as speakers.

If you do not see that over time, your grade moves from pass to fail. Your diverse talent should have a clear track upward. This is a recurring problem in many industries. Not everyone you hire wants to be or should be in a leadership role, but what are you doing to foster and develop the talent who do?

Having diverse talent adds to your bottom line and fosters innovation. Determine if your firm will be a leader in your industry for diversity and inclusion or miss out on promoting a talented group of employees. Again, this responsibility rests on each team member. Having a seat at the table is critical. This signals to the entire company that representation matters. Always remember one rule of thumb, inclusive is inclusive. If your business is not diverse and inclusive, then you are doing something wrong.

4. Affinity Groups

Affinity groups signal another intentional step toward creating a more diverse and inclusive workplace. An affinity group is a group of individuals generally underrepresented in the larger culture who are linked together by a commonality or a purpose. Affinity groups can comprise people of color, women, or LGBTQ employees, among others. If your company employs any underrepresented groups that do not have a support system in place, this is an intentional way to create an inclusive environment.

The Memo has conducted workshops for affinity groups of color at Fortune 500 companies. I am always impressed when companies take the time to create affinity groups and invest resources to help their employees thrive. Affinity groups can serve as a professional development tool and provide networking opportunities for your employees. This is a chance for them to create community with staff they can identify with. Relationship and community-building is essential when creating an environment for inclusivity.

When our firm conducts workshops for affinity groups, we focus on ways to help each team acquire and enhance their skillset. For example, one popular workshop is on how to craft your elevator pitch. If you are a small firm, you might not have the budget to pull off providing frequent professional development opportunities, so start small. Host a talk, workshop, or lunch-and-learn once a quarter. Alternatively, sponsor your diverse talent to attend conferences, workshops, or seminars that would be mutually beneficial to their work and professional development. These opportunities provide outlets for your employees to thrive; thriving talent is retained talent, and supported talent will reflect their happiness in their output and your bottom line.

Try and put yourself in your talent's shoes: If you were part of an underrepresented group, what tools would you need to succeed?

5. Overcoming Unconscious Bias

What is unconscious bias? The University of California, San Francisco defines it as social stereotypes about particular groups of people that individuals form outside their own conscious awareness. Everyone holds unconscious beliefs about various social and identity groups; these biases stem from one's tendency to organize social worlds by categorizing. Once I joined a new team, and a colleague asked me if they hired me to handle all the black clients. I would like to think my colleague didn't mean any harm, but regardless of her intention, this is a form of unconscious bias. I was not tasked to handle the black clients any more than anyone else on our team. I replied by letting her know that I was hired because of my talent and ability to engage all clients.

Let's reverse the conversation; I would never think to ask a colleague if they were employed for one sole reason. And at this particular organization, there was no affirmative action. Certain words and behaviors that might come out of your mouth may be well-intentioned, but the effect is that the receiver may deem it offensive and borderline racist. This is why having the right benchmarks and training is key to streamline the amount of unconscious bias.

For example, take two resumes; one's applicant's name is Jerome and the other's is Jack. Right off the bat, you are going to assume Jerome is an African-American male. But, many men in the South (during a period of time) were named Jerome regardless of race. As another example, take a pregnant woman interviewing for a job. You might automatically assume several stereotypes regarding expectant mothers. Some hiring managers might see this as a problem, while others might view this as a win. But, if a man interviews and mentions that his wife/partner is six months pregnant, it doesn't stop the show.

Unconscious bias, in my opinion, is the gateway drug to microaggressions. Microaggressions by definition are subtle forms of prejudice. Neither are award-winning behaviors, and as someone who has experienced both on several occasions, I can say that it's something no employee should encounter in the workplace. These attitudes run rampant throughout some companies, and you should establish a zero-tolerance policy for this type of behavior. It is one surefire way to diminish all the work you are creating to be more inclusive.

Again, to this kind of workforce, you must communicate from the top down. In my own career, my experiences of unconscious bias came straight from the senior leaders. I don't believe they were aware of their behavior, but there was never an environment in which I felt safe to address my concerns. I went years just pushing through uncomfortable situations. Your leadership is responsible for change.

Diversity and inclusion is a long game. The culture cannot shift overnight, but you must implement steps now so the future of your company can sustain a diverse talent pool. Use these five steps as your metric and benchmarks.

I suggest to my clients implementing 30-, 60-, and 90-day plans. If you already have a robust D&I department, what can you do to take it to the next level? How can you support your diverse talent going forward? You have the power to change the ratio by taking meaningful, thoughtful, and strategic steps toward change. Doing nothing is not an option.

What are you going to do to make your industry more inclusive?

Minda Harts is the founder and CEO of The Memo LLC, a premier career development platform for women of color. The Memo helps women of color prepare for their seat at the table with education, community, and access. Additionally, The Memo conducts career workshops for Fortune 500 companies to enhance their diversity and inclusion initiatives. Minda has been featured in Essence Magazine, The Huffington Post, NBC News, and the Guardian. She also serves as a mentor at General Assembly.

CHAPTER 5

Technology + Transparency = Transformation

In *The Radical CPA*, I explain the cloud and how it works. However, I've always maintained that the hows are not important.

What's critical to understand is that cloud firms require a new type of management. Why? Because the cloud is disruptive to CPA firms' core management philosophies. The cloud disrupts what we're selling.

The most important thing I want you to remember is that technology becomes part of the products you sell. This is a totally different way of looking at technology in a CPA firm. In a traditional firm, technology is a tool or piece of overhead. In today's New Firm, technology is part of what we sell. It becomes part of the product.

This is a huge change in thinking.

In *The Radical CPA* I wrote about how I categorize my technology costs as product costs, or as part of a cost of goods sold. Why is this so important?

It's important because it truly becomes one of the inputs of what you're selling. And as you productize your services, you will selectively choose the right technology that you will resell as part of your solution. When we get to pricing, it will become important that you bundle your technology fees with your solutions. If you do not, it becomes too easy for your customer to try and pick apart your solution. You do not want to give customers the option of working with you differently. It's too easy for a customer to say, "I don't need that technology because of the cost" when they don't understand that the technology allows for the transparency as well as the capacity within the CPA firm. It is unrealistic for a firm to have 300 ways of doing something. It will not scale and it will frustrate your team.

And remember, you are not selling a service, you are selling a solution.

That solution includes technology chosen for that specific customer. This is key to understanding how you will continue to adopt new technologies and how you will sell your firm's solutions. The idea of this technology being sold as part of the solution allows for capacity, process, and a uniform way of doing accounting for multiple customers. Without this uniformity, it is extremely difficult to scale. This is why old-school firms are caught in the rat race of everything being done differently. It is only in solution-selling that customers buy the technology you choose for them. Everyone must utilize the same trial balance or system. For example, you can't walk into our firm with an Excel spreadsheet and have an expectation of a tax return. You need to be on our system. We sell business and tax solutions, not numbers entered on tax returns.

> You can't walk into our firm with an Excel spreadsheet and have an expectation of a tax return. You need to be on our system. We sell business and tax solutions, not numbers entered on tax returns.

In today's world, I would argue that in any given month I can find a new technology that will automate my process and deliver better value for my firm. It is because of this that I believe product management is the way to help facilitate ongoing technology. And you don't have to be the only one who introduces new technology. Remember our trusty friends the Millennials? They are exceptional at this stuff. But anyone on your team can find a new tool—it's not an age thing.

Customizing Technology For Your Customer

When you know your customer well, you can then map out your specific services and technologies for them while considering their needs and goals and technological ability.

For example, in our solution for graphic designers, we include FreshBooks as well as QuickBooks Online. The reason being is we know our graphic designers only are concerned with invoicing (remember our persona exercise) and FreshBooks has one of the simpler invoicing products out there. We don't confuse our graphic designers and try and teach them Intuit invoicing when we know FreshBooks is a product that better meets their needs.

However, as accountants, we also need a balance sheet, and so we use Quick-

Books Online for that piece of the solution. Our graphic designers don't care because we are not selling them software. All the software fees are included in our monthly price for that; all they care about is that the interface is easy and we picked the best-of-breed invoicing for the task. It's not helpful to your customer to have them use a solution that doesn't meet their needs. That is why it is so important to figure out what is going to go into the solution or productized services you are selling and why knowing your customer is critical.

Therefore, knowing the cloud and all the products available because of cloud technologies is so important. If you don't know what is available and on the market, how can you best serve your customers?

It's time to productize your services and use the cloud with all your customers, not just one or two. If you allow that to happen, your firm will go through a transformation. A transformation that can't be taken lightly; a transformation that will give you more capacity to do more—whether that includes adopting more technology, taking on more client work, or focusing on growth and business development.

The Wonderful World of Apps

This idea of using a productized service allows for a whole app ecosystem. It allows us as the accountants to select and create the complete office system for our customers. We now can help them select a cloud-driven application program that allows them to run their business and connect it to the general ledger system. As opposed to the old way, when we tried to make the accounting system do all of their other business processes as well. Now, the business recording and operational piece takes part in the app program and only the accounting gets done in the accounting program. We also now have the opportunity to perform functions like invoicing, accounts receivable, and account payable remotely for the functions to increasingly become a critical part of their accounting team. Hello stickiness factor!

Every day, more functional apps are being included to help small business run better. In the small business sector, both the Intuit and Xero app stores are growing. And Sage Live lives in the Salesforce ecosystem, taking you upstream to the next level of customer.

The app store also includes apps to allow for small business lending—both traditional and alternative types of lending—as well as the ability to receive a cash advance on a specific receivable. Have you ever heard of Fundbox? Are you aware of how you can add value to customers when you have a complete understanding of the technology that is accessible to them in a cloud world? How about using technology to facilitate cash flow consulting engagements?

It is important that you work in tandem with your customers on these initiatives to standardize operations and streamline internal controls. It's also critical that you have a solid grasp of your internal team to help them implement and even do daily processing as needed. It is critical to your firm and its internal workflows. If you let your customers lead the way, you will end up no better than you were before your transformation as too many options become overwhelming to your team. We are looking to build efficiencies and create repeatable product sales to other customers, not sell hourly time consulting for one-off jobs.

Another issue I have seen happen is overkill. Make sure you have the correct system for the correct level of work. When looking at options, it is so important to make sure the technology fits the business and that it's the right size for them today with a roadmap for growth in the future. Too many times the solution does not fit the need.

The New Vision way: The Cloud At Work

As a Radical CPA, you already know the cloud allows you to work anytime, anywhere. By adopting the cloud, you can connect to all your data via an Internet browser or an app. You can work on almost any device.

It's a pretty brilliant invention.

My firm uses the CCH Axcess suite and Office 365 for tax work. This combination allows us to be server-free.

Yes, you read right.

No. Server. Anywhere.

Our clients use QuickBooks Online, Xero, or Sage Live. If you want to work with our firm you need to be using one of those products.

Setting this requirement has allowed us to standardize our processes and streamline our work. As a result, it has created an exponential amount of capacity because everything is bank-feed driven. What does that mean? It means that our our bank statement fetcher Hubdoc allows us to connect directly to our customer accounts so we don't have to bug them every time we need that access.

Making It All Look Easy

Let's be honest, technology is not easy. Yes, it makes our lives easier, but by itself it's not easy. You must choose it. You must learn it. You must implement it. You must use it. And when your firm's livelihood depends on it, it can make you bananas. Add in that it's always changing, and, well, it gets complicated.

How do you stay on top of it all?

R&D is required!

There needs to be some clarification here about technology and technology.

Yes, that's exactly what I said.

Today's technology mindset is different—we are utilizing the Internet to essentially solve problems.

Too many owners think of technology as IT, as in, there's a server in the back room and everyone needs to stay away from it. Today's technology mindset is different—we are utilizing the Internet to essentially solve problems. And the answers are at our fingertips.

You no longer need an IT expert to solve your accounting IT solution problems.

Sorry, IT people!

What you need within your firm is a superb researcher.

Just like in tax, when you have an issue or question come up, you charge someone on the tax team to go see if they can find the answer. You already know that any answer from yesterday may not be the answer in two weeks due to tax law changes or court case rulings.

It's the exact same idea applied to technology. You define the problem or the issue, and then you send a team member to the Internet to look for solutions. You gather a few solutions, download some trials, or do a few demos. You read a few reviews. You connect with other CPAs in forums such as LinkedIn and ask them if they'd use these products. You test them on your own firm. And then you decide. Products are coming out so frequently that you can't even wait for formal reviews.

Every firm, no matter how small, should have this research and development (R&D) component. What I found is that firms that embrace technology have exponentially more capacity to embrace more technology. The easiest way to find out about new technologies is to talk to other CPAs and other small business owners and learn what they are using. We also need to be constantly scanning our environment, both inside our industry and outside our industry, for new opportunities in technology. A good place to find new technologies is at technology trade shows within the industry or via online research. Google, anyone?

R&D to me is using a new technology to see how it works, either on a customer or with your team. Too often technology does not actually work the way you would think it should. Yes, sometimes the process needs to change to work with the technology. However, often, what is sold does not match what is there (sorry vendors, just speaking the truth here). I believe the only way to refer products is to be able to use them firsthand.

If this technology is going to become part of multiple solutions that you sell to your customers, you roll it out once, then twice, and then yet again to see how it functions and if you like it. If you do great then you roll it out across your product line. If you don't, you go and look for another solution to solve for that problem.

If the technology is going to be specially implemented on one customer, be transparent with them. Let them know that you haven't used this solution before, but that you have implemented many other similar solutions and you will be able to troubleshoot your way through the implementation. This is where pricing comes into play, because you may not know the full scope, but I will talk more about that later, in the value chapter.

You'll absolutely need technology to create your product. Again, this gets to the mindset of what are we selling, and that's a productized service.

At New Vision, our technology spend is close 15 to 20 percent. The cost of technology replaces labor. Not a bad thing in the tough talent market.

Talk about changes in technology with your customer.

Technology brings about business transformation.

You're an accountant—you're not in the technology sales business. You are in the business solutions business, or what I like to call the business transformation business.

Oh wait, you thought because you're an accountant, you're in the accounting business? This is changing. I would caution you that computers and robots will be doing all the accounting in the very near future. I'm not trying to scare you, but we need to evolve our business.

After all, the business we're in is bigger than accounting. Accounting is one piece of the entire pie. Now that we have the cloud we can offer so much more: strategic planning, CFO outsourcing, consulting, tax planning, wealth management. We can create a platform that addresses all our customer's financial needs with a variety of carefully chosen products that make it all feel easy.

When we're with the customer, we typically don't talk about technology. We talk about solving problems. But what I have found is that when I talk about solving problems, technology just naturally pops its head into the conversation. A great thing about technology is that it's getting easier and more user-friendly. More people understand its power and capabilities. Sometimes, if I run across an issue, I ask my teenage son to show me how to use it first.

Name the tech-savvy person in your firm, charge them with technology R&D, and watch the innovation happen.

Using technology means always learning.

You've finally finished implementing a new system. You finally get it. It took sweat. It took resources. It took teamwork to the 10th degree. You feel proud.

Your employees are high off the win. Your customers think it's cool. And then some new app or tool crosses your path and it's shiny and new and you want to check it out! Like as soon as possible!

Isn't that always the way?

When I was figuring this out, I was always asking, is there a way to make technology changes part of our firm culture? How can I embrace and own the fact that technology is always changing, and since I pride myself in being a tech junkie, how can I keep up and enjoy it?

News flash: We can no longer wait five years to update technology. And yes, I'm talking about computers. New technologies come out continuously, and they improve our process exponentially. Therefore, we must make it part of our DNA to be always looking, always challenging, and always thinking about our process and how our technology can make it faster.

It's constant learning!

How to Talk to Vendors About Technology

Rule number 1: Do not talk to the sales guys.

Find a product manager.

Hey, remember, this is what we are learning to be! Product managers love to talk to customers, and usually they understand their products so well that they know what their limitations are as well as the problems they are solving.

Where do you find a product manager?

Usually live product managers are out and about on a trade show floor. Otherwise, if you get the sales person ask them to refer you to the product manager. Feel free to challenge the product manager with features and functionality that you would like to see.

Product managers love this.

Keep an eye out: what in the &$@* are AI and bots?

Are you ready? Because we're Radical 2.0 and we're going beyond bank feeds. The reason being is that technology is automating everything faster. Soon we will be using artificial intelligence and bots to do accounting.

Artificial intelligence (AI) is intelligence exhibited by machines.

Does that freak you out?

It should if you perceive your value in producing a financial statement instead of doing something proactive or advisory.

We all say we're proactive and advisory.

Those are probably two of the most overused words in our profession. But to be real, you should know that accounting vendors have already started to use bots and show their value. They are automating simple tasks and getting smarter every day. The world is moving so quickly that we need to have a rapid prototyping way of incorporating all this new technology into what our firms sell every day. That is why our R&D is so important to the New Firm model.

One type of AI is called a bot. What is a bot? According to Kurt Wagner's article for Recode, "Bots, Explained," a bot is software that is designed to automate the kinds of tasks you would usually do on your own—like making a dinner reservation, adding an appointment to your calendar, or fetching and displaying information. Wagner says we're hearing more about them because AI software is improving dramatically as a result of attention from Facebook and Google.

My favorite bot is Digit. This bot basically gives me a recap of my banking transactions and incrementally saves small amounts by moving money from my checking account to my savings account. I can text it and it responds back. It's quicker than an app and it's smarter, too.

Thoughts on AI From Sage AI VP Kriti Sha

Kriti Sharma, vice president of AI and bots at Sage, said this in response to Digit:

"As an industry, we need to be more careful about that. It's not just moving money from one account to another. The second point I would say is design. It's a very important element of this. We see people sometimes like to have more control.

"Like with AI, we can tailor the experience. You might be the kind of [accountant] who does not want the bot to ask [your customer], "Do you want me to remind you?" The accountant might be the kind of customer who does want . . . to ask the bot, "Do it for me." The accountant could be the person who wants to do that final approval, yes or no, and we can tailor that experience for individual users. That is the power that we did not have with Google apps, that functionality. But AI can be a personal assistant, which works wonderfully."

Sharma's team also built Pegg, (the Sage bot). It is fairly simple now with the accounting functions—it can record an income or expense—but it's learning fast. He commented:

"We wanted to be the personal trainer for businesses. Think of a personal trainer for your health and fitness that's helping you do well. If your finances are not doing well, this is what you should and shouldn't to do, and it's specific for you. We can create a financial assistant like that to help you modify those things."

The vendors are all creating their own bots to be part of their accounting software. Think about telling Pegg (the Sage bot) to make a journal entry for you instead of logging in to do it. We didn't know how Siri or Alexa would change our lives, and now we will have the innovations in our accounting journals.

Blockchain: The Basics

Historically, when it comes to transacting money or anything of value, people and businesses have relied heavily on intermediaries like banks and governments to ensure trust and certainty.

Middlemen perform a range of important tasks that help build trust into the transactional process like authentication and record keeping.

Blockchain changes this.

Blockchain is a type of distributed ledger or decentralized database that keeps records of digital transactions. Rather than having a central administrator like a traditional database (think banks, governments, and accountants), a distributed ledger has a network of replicated databases, synchronized via the Internet and visible to anyone within the network. Blockchain networks can be private, with restricted membership similar to an intranet, or public, like the Internet, accessible to any person in the world.

This distributed ledger can exponentially reduce the need for accountants and will change banking as we know it.

Currently, a program built with Blockchain is already disrupting the payment space with a service called Veem that can transfer money overseas for only an exchange fee. No bank wire needed! It doesn't take long to get set up. It is saving small businesses thousands of dollars in transaction fees.

Are you aware of it? Should you be? This is an everyday example of how technology is changing how we serve our customers. A practical approach where we can look like a shero.

Do you have customers who are banks? Have you discussed these new technologies with them? If not, why not?

As many talk about the evil of technology reducing our jobs, I look toward the positive to see how to use the technology to add value to my firm and our customers.

CHAPTER 6

Maximizing Social Media and Product Marketing & the Importance of People

Social media is the underdog of business development. Although I build relationships in both an offline and the online world, most my firm's business comes directly from having both an online and an offline connection. I have multiple clients now who I have never met IRL (in real life).

It's all about relationships; it always has been

Customer service has always been about relationships—whether responding to an email, returning a phone call, or meeting the customer for lunch. However, in today's online world, one must include social media as an everyday conversation tool. This tool also needs to be part of our productized services and what we are selling. If it is not, we are losing an opportunity to connect with the next generation business owner. Social business takes many forms. It could be content driven, like a podcast, or it could be a relationship connection on Facebook or LinkedIn.

Most of you already know this by now, but in the new world of social selling, the more a potential customer gets to know you via blogs or podcasts, the more likely they are going to do business with you. They understand you and who you are. They feel like they know you, and that's why it's easier for them to decide to work with you.

Social selling is lead generation rooted in social media. Right now, there are buyers all over the world who want to buy your solutions. They have a need, they have a timeframe for purchase, they even have budget. If only you could get in front of them, they'd buy from you right now.

At New Vision, and at other Radical firms across the United States, we are in front of them because we live and breathe in places on the Internet where they frequent. And we've proven to them that we have the expertise to solve their problem.

The Radical Way to Finding Out More About Your Customer

It can be overwhelming when you think about all the ways to connect via social media. Instagram. Snapchat. Periscope. Facebook. LinkedIn. Twitter. And that's only a handful of mediums. While it can be overwhelming, it's also a vast opportunity to gather information on the people you work with and the people you want to work with. It's in this opportunity that you can offer additional value to your customers.

Now, I know you can't be everywhere all the time.

However, if just 10 percent of the time you can catch something new and special from one of your relationships online, your relationships will automatically get stronger. The opportunity to build stronger relationships via online is easier than meeting someone for coffee or lunch.

Earlier in this book we talked about personas; personas are important from a marketing and business development perspective. But how do you find out more about your customers? Find them online! Find out their likes and dislikes, who they follow, and the connections you share. Discover what their style is like and who they admire. You can get a lot of information about people online.

Who are your Facebook friends?

Are you friends with your customers and vendors on Facebook? I am. I believe that Facebook is one is the easiest platforms on which to maintain relationships. It is through pictures of what they eat and their kids, and through the silly things they post that you can get to know your customers better.

For example, one of our largest customers is my friend on Facebook. I saw that he had the opportunity to go golfing with Arnold Palmer. The next time I saw him I asked him how that came to be. We could connect on a deeper level. I didn't even have to go golfing.

You can't just lurk on Facebook. If you're going to use Facebook as a relationship building tool, you'll need to share information about yourself and you'll need to respond to your customers' posts.

How to Negotiate Boundaries In a Social, Mobile World

The concept of working and being available all the time is exhausting, and just not possible. But the expectation is there. The problem with social business is not the "how to use" piece, but in having to negotiate boundaries with people who want your attention all the time!

The bottom line is: It's a personal, somewhat generational, choice. You get to decide how accessible you want to be, how available you can be, and how you ultimately want to communicate.

However, I strongly recommend you think about this carefully and figure out how to meet your customers and vendors where they are without sacrificing your sustainability or sanity.

It's one of the hardest things you'll have to manage about being social.

Boundaries in a Social/Mobile World

Here are some of my tips on setting boundaries in the social world.

- Be upfront with your customers. If I respond immediately—awesome, however on social I may not respond immediately.
- Develop rules for yourself. Do you really want to respond at 10:30pm, and is it the smartest thing for you to do?
- Stick to your rules.
- Set clear expectations with your team. Communicate them.

Think about coverage… what are the expectations for your teams, and what are they watching from a customer service perspective?

I would argue that you need to give customers some access. The global companies that have figured out how to do social business are killing it. Social has also become a customer service channel; you will need to discover the boundaries you want to set there, too. Today's customer expects to have access to your business via social. It is this expectation that creates disruption to a firm. However, if you can put this social channel of customer service into a productized service that you're selling, it becomes easier to figure out its boundaries. I'm 100 percent me online and offline. I share a lot, but I'm a pretty open person in the real world as well. I've found that being authentic works for me.

Top 20 Social Media Hacks to Build Your Business

By Becky Livingston

Social media should be a major part of your business marketing plan.

Here are 20 ideas to help you build your small business.

You can use many of these ideas on one or more platforms; they are all designed to help increase engagement, develop leads, and grow your brand.

1. Use hashtags. Hashtagify.me is a great tool to help you find relevant hashtags for your client industries, your service lines, and content topics. It can also help you find influencers and to see the conversations already taking place around a hashtag. Remember, when you're creating a hashtag, look it up first to make sure it's not being used in a conversation you do not want your brand associated with.

2. Boost your productivity with scheduling tools. Hootsuite, Buffer, and dlvr.it help you preschedule posts so you're not tied to your computer. Social media is not a set-it-and-forget-it tool. You must engage, comments, share, and post to be effective.

3. Generate new content ideas with AnswerThePublic.com, where you can see what questions the public is asking about a given topic. For example, if you enter "business audit," you will see questions like "What does a business audit mean?", "What is audit business risk?", and "What does a business audit consist of?" All of these are great topics for blog content and white papers.

4. Use graphics in all social media posts. Canva (canva.com) is a free, easy to use way to create beautiful graphics for the major social media platforms. It's also great for presentation graphics, booklet covers, brochures, online ads, and more.

5. Spend a few dollars to increase your social media reach on Facebook, Twitter, and LinkedIn posts, some platforms charge as little as $5 to boost your posts, expanding your reach outside your existing follower base.

6. Increase Twitter's 140-character limit using this trick: Type a tweet as you normally would, but end it with an ellipse (. . .) or cliffhanger or some kind. Then reply to your own tweet in your Twitter stream, but remove the mention of your name, and keep typing. Watch this video for more on this tip >> https://www.youtube.com/watch?v=OJRp22IXqXY.

7. Avoid the dreaded LinkedIn blocked profile with this Google search hack. Let's

say you're looking for leads located in Indiana who mention "restaurant" in their profiles. Go to Google's search box and type in site:linkedin.com "restaurant" Indiana. You should get search results of people who've mentioned the term in their profile, as well as other LinkedIn content and groups associated with that term.

8. Get a hand writing social content. It can be tedious to create multiple tweets from the same blog article; Missinglettr.com offers you a solution. For just $15/month for a personal account, or $40/month for a business account, the tool will create social media content based on your blog content—and it will schedule that content over the course of the year. It integrates with Twitter, LinkedIn, GooglePlus, and Facebook.

9. Install the Click To Tweet plugin on your WordPress site. Then when writing content, you can add clickable moments that your readers can share quickly. No typing needed on their part, and your handle is included in the repost.

10. Listen in on others' social conversations. This is just as important as posting. If you're not listening to the conversation, how do you get involved? Hootsuite, TweetReach, Social Mention, HowSociable, and other tools will help you discover the who, what, where, why, when, and how around the topics others are talking about.

11. Filter comments based on keywords in Instagram. This is a great way to organize comments by keyword, particularly if you've experienced trolls on your account. You can filter by comments or even turn off offenders. Here's how: In your account, click on the gear icon; choose Comments; then toggle the Hide Inappropriate Comments option.

12. Use UTM parameters in your URLs to track clicks from various media to your website. Do this by searching for URL builders. Then complete the website URL by adding campaign source (such as blog); campaign medium (such as Facebook); and campaign content, which is the main phrase for your content. Here's an example: http://www.newvisioncpagroup.com/services/?utm_source=website&utm_medium=Facebook&utm_content=radical-services. Then put the long URL in a URL shortener or your social media scheduling tool. Later, in your analytics, you'll be able to see from where people are entering your site and from which piece of content, not just from which platform.

13. Save time with social media robot If This, Then That (IFTTT). Here's how it works: Connect your social media profiles, blog, cell phone, etc. Then create the array of

things you want to happen. You can have it simultaneously update your Twitter profile image whenever you update your Facebook profile image. Or, you can have it email you your favorite tweets. Or, you can tell it to store your Instagram photos in your Dropbox account.

14. Create Twitter lists targeting your posts to industry influencers, thought leaders who might share your content, and/or your target audience. Once you create a list, your targeted tweet would look like this: @username/listname (make sure there are no spaces in your list name; you can use dashes.

15. Rather than simply posting your firm videos to YouTube, create a channel, so that when someone views your videos, they do not see other users' video content on the sidebar.

16. Keep track of your firm's content posts in Excel or other tool, then repurpose those posts throughout the year to draw in new readers and potential leads. This helps you save time since it's content you've already created.

17. Tie a blog to a trending topic or television show. For example, as Mother's Day or Father's Day approaches, ask staff about the best advice their parents gave them and then make a blog or video from their responses. Haiku Deck and SlideTeam. net have some stunning visuals you can use to create slide decks that you can then easily transform into a video.

18. Use listening streams to stay on top of trending topics your clients and firm. If you're using a social media scheduling tool, such as Hootsuite, create a stream just for an industry, like #Construction. That stream will collect any posts containing that hashtag, which saves you time when you're looking for content to share. It also helps you find both your influencers and your competition.

19. Implement contests, sweepstakes, and landing pages into your Facebook marketing initiative with 22Social (22social.com). This fee-based tool connects to your company page and helps you create professional-looking events, promo pages, giveaway and sweepstakes pages, podcast promo pages, digital courses, and more.

20. Extend your firm's SEO and personal influence ranking using the LinkedIn publishing platform. First, make sure your firm is listed as your employer on your LinkedIn profile. Next, write original content on the Publish page. Remember to use a keyword in the title, in the image filename you load with the piece, and in the copy. This is most helpful if you're creating blog content for your firm already

and repurposing that on your LinkedIn profile. Then share it in groups where your target audience hangs out and on your personal profile.

Becky Livingston is the founder and CEO of Penheel Marketing. She has more than 20 years of experience in marketing and communications, as well as a strong background in technology. She can also be found doing public speaking gigs across the country.

Marketing Innovation: Experiment and Take Risks

Eric Majchrzak is a shareholder and the chief marketing officer of BeachFleischman PC, a Top 200 firm in Tucson, Arizona, with approximately about $28 million in revenue, 21 partners, and 160 employees. We go way back. He's been known to be pioneering when it comes to digital marketing and social media. I asked him what he's been up to lately; this is how he responded:

Most of the things that we're innovating right now have to do with disrupted marketing techniques and strategies, so we're moving into and pushing into a larger market, like Phoenix.

In terms of our size, we're pretty small in Phoenix, compared to all those other firms, so we have to do things that disrupt, that create our own space.

In other words, we can't run a traditional marketing campaign out there.

It has to be something that's asymmetric almost. We like to test different things.

Example 1: We're the first company in Phoenix to publish content on the "Phoenix Business Journal" website. It's a beta program. We're the only company right now that's in there. It's category exclusive, but we get to post our thought leadership on their site since we have a hub content file. We're pushing that content out, and then they push that content out to their readers, to their daily email, their social channels, and then on the website itself.

Example 2: A creative partnership that we've developed with a media outlet in Phoenix, that's an NPR radio affiliate. We just struck a content licensing agreement with them where they are providing our firm with co-branded business content that's Arizona-specific. They have a news desk of business reporters in Arizona reporting on the economy of Arizona, different industry verticals, so we struck a deal with them where they're giving us their content, and now we are essentially an extension of an NPR radio affiliate. We are exclusively publishing their content, podcasts, blog posts, and images. We are sponsoring the mobile app because of it. It's creating our own space and a lot of times it's an exchange. We'll be able to provide them with seminars for their listeners and their donors and things. It's a big, collaborative partnership. It's not simply just like a media buy.

Example 3: Arizona State University. We approached their not-for-profit think tank. It's part of the university. It's called the Lodestar Center and that's the college for not-for-profit professionals. They have a professional development center, which is for professionals that are already in the industry working, like executive directors and CFOs of not-for-profits, and we bought the naming rights to their non-profit management certificate program.

Other firms can't do that because, again, they're regional. They don't have marketing professionals . . . on the ground [who are] really focused on growing that market per se as much as they are just doing support, almost administrative support, where we can be more strategic and more deliberative and disruptive, really.

It's creating our own space, separating ourselves, and aligning ourselves with large, institutional, credible brands, and that's how we're going to cut through the clutter and grow.

Marketing Changes… are you ready?

Product marketing is so different than selling a service hours. It's easier to teach to your employees.

Why? Because there are advantages to selling a product.

Product solutions offer a uniform solution to customers' problems. If you sell product solutions, you sell identical versions to numerous customers. You may offer advanced or improved versions of products, but even those remain very similar to each other. Your prospects can evaluate features before they buy, and if you do not sell to one prospect, you can try to sell the same item to another prospect. When you sell a product, you can focus more on selling than on customizing the product. If you are unable to explain your business and know the value of what you sell then it doesn't matter what you sell.

If we're selling correctly, we're ultimately anchored in the customer's "gap." The gap between where they are today and where they want to be tomorrow. We're selling based on solving measurable, tangible, urgent business problems.

Also, if we have customized our personas correctly, the customer naturally wants to buy because the product fits them and it is sold as such. As opposed to us saying, "I am a CPA and I can help you with accounting and tax." What does that even mean?

Is there a defined outcome or a deliverable that is tangible and valuable to a customer beside a compliance based document?

Of course.

But I would argue that our customers are not convinced based on our poor sales process. If we were good at defining and delivering on value, our fees would not be subject to the scrutiny they currently are today. The value would be apparent.

It's also easier for the team to understand the value gap; when they do, they can better explain it and ultimately sell it.

They also begin to understand their value, and how to step back and say, this work is above and beyond the original scope, and to price for it separately and potentially define a new product offering. It's just easier to sell a complete solution rather than a billable hour of time that has no defined end.

When you productize your offering, it is easier to sell in a channel. When you define and create channel sales you have the opportunity to grow faster due to those channel sales. Referrals are always good, but isn't it exponentially better to receive referrals from a technology channel partner? When you have a productized service offering, you can develop thought leadership within that technology vendor's channel.

That can greatly increase your sales much quicker than one-off referrals. And because you have standardized everything, it is easy to assimilate this growth into your firm due to all the processes you have created for your specific offerings.

Selling to niches becomes easier as well because your persona matches perfectly to the niches' needs. When you can match their exact need, speak in their words, and bring the solution to their problem, that becomes a powerful growth option. Add a little thought leadership, show up where the customer lives both online and offline, and not only can you sell your solution, you can increase its price as well, because a specialist can always command a higher price than a generalist based on value and expertise.

The choice becomes yours if you want to only serve a specific niche and create a boutique firm.

Yay team!

Capacity gives you and your team incredible opportunities for professional growth. Never at any of my old-school firm jobs did I feel like I was part of a team.

Yes, I had co-workers who would help if needed.

But it was always at the expense of an hour. That may seem harsh, but if your managers are looking at budget hours and you need coaching to get through your part of the assignment, they might only offer up their help begrudgingly.

There is no team play in a billable hour model.

Hours by their inherent nature are an individual sport.

Take away the tracking of time and running a firm differently creates a whole new level of learning. You're constantly learning new tools, learning via new technical CPE, and, most importantly, learning from the team around you. You're learning new tech from the Millennial who holds your hand as you figure out a different way to document something.

Why is it they know all the drag-and-drop tips?

You can have the bandwidth now to spend extra time to fully explain why you do a specific task—and not just to more inexperienced team members. Or even explain the history of a certain tax code. I love watching the lightbulb come on, or, even better, hearing team members explain it to a customer.

You can now teach across roles so that more team members know different aspects of all the jobs, not just their specific part.

Everybody has to step up their game in teaching and delegating to other team members.

This is the hard part, as we have had little in the way of learning how to manage work and people. Managing work is very different than collecting and billing time. It's a completely new skill set. New Firms really feel like a team sport. They have to, in order to survive. They experience exponential growth, which forces the firms and its members to sink or swim.

And oh, how they are swimming!

Time tracking will need to eventually go away for New Firms due to the above. It has to! But incrementally. If you can manage work, and set realistic expectations that team members can easily understand and accomplish, and allow for some leeway if you absolutely must track time as a stepping stone, you are well on your way to a culture of learning and vast growth.

Get in the (Work) Flow

If you are not already using workflow software you absolutely must start using it now. This is the easiest way to manage work. Which is what you should be managing in your firm instead of time. There are various workflow products out there, and they have different purposes. Some may integrate with your tax software, and some may only do accounting or other project management. I'm even aware of firms using workflow software not specific to the accounting industry. If you can manage your work it should help you manage your people. Also, you need to look at and appropriately allocate capacity. I have yet to find the perfect tool for capacity management.

Try it out and start here:
- Find/create a group or service area within a larger firm that does mostly fixed pricing.
- Manage work, not time.
- Utilize workflow software to measure delivery dates, time in house, turnaround time, etc.
- See how it works.
- Roll out across firm.
- Have party.

Love Your People: Encouraging Responsibility, Growing Leaders

Where is ownership and leadership in the old-school model?

Uh, nowhere?

Is that why everyone is complaining there is no one left to take over our firms anymore? Whose fault is that?

In a New Firm model, leadership evolves naturally because team members are forced to grow (aka get out of their comfort zones). The learning is constant and firms are growing organically.

It's on-the-job leader training.

The New Firms are growing very quickly and, quite frankly, hiring from the outside doesn't work due to the "old firm mentality" that has been drilled into younger staff people today.

In the old model, leaders get burnt out and leave for corporate opportunities. The grunt work is pushed down to new team members. In the New Firms, the grunt work is done by technology, and team members are forced into customer service and customer questions or advisory work much sooner.

This makes for an engaged team.

You will also see a customer service role evolve. Although it is based in administrative, like procedures, it is more than an administrative assistant. I used to say it was a digital admin, but it's actually more. This customer service role become critical in growing your firm. It will make you rethink training, which becomes an everyday occurrence in the New Firm model. The good thing is that we now have capacity for all this training because we aren't billing for hours. We can teach each other.

Consider this: An easy step on the road to no longer tracking time might be to allocate a certain number of hours to learning that is not CPE driven. A certain number of hours to "customer work." A certain number of hours to customer service. Before you know it, your team will naturally evolve. Ultimately, work still needs to be produced, but when you aren't tracking the minutes, your team can learn to lead itself. The folks who aren't capable will be exposed, and you can coach them or remove them from your firm. Most likely you already know who they are anyway. The stars will shine brighter and you can give them more opportunities to grow as your firm changes and moves through its transformation.

This is my favorite part of the transformation. I am so proud of a truly working-in-a-team model. It's not always easy, but it's a much more sustainable and happy model for both professional and personal growth.

CHAPTER 7
Name Your Price

The Unavoidable: The Power Struggle Between Succession & Partner Compensation

I'm going to address the elephant in the room. Ready? It's succession and how it relates to partner compensation. I can give you many reasons why time and billing is no longer relevant. I can give you the reasons why customers want fixed or value-based prices.

However, until I tell you how your partner compensation is going to be impacted, you will not change.

If I was sitting in the retiring partner seat, I'm not sure how I would feel about all these transformative changes happening to today's firm. I have my own experience because I've been through a succession. But it was from the other side. It was about taking over my dad's firm. However, his firm was relatively small. Most of our substantial growth came from new business I created, not from his legacy customers.

Believe me when I tell you that we had many power struggles over how to change things or why not to change. But because of my strong personality and his willingness to let me make my own mistakes, the succession was successful. Yet, it was not easy. So, I've been there. I know what it's like to be on one side of the table. And I would like to think that I have compassion and empathy for what it must be like sitting on the other side of the table.

That said, for firms to be sustainable, changes must occur. Young partners absolutely want to invest in growth and R&D and in doing things differently. Growth takes money because it involves risk. It takes an investment of both energy and cash. The partner who is retiring is thinking, "I just want to maintain the status quo so I can get my payout; I've been here long enough, and I want to retire because growth is not important to me anymore." Ouch.

I know that sounds harsh, but we all know this is happening. It's the state of our aging profession.

Yet the young partner sees the future and wants to invest. They know they will have to be working for at least another 20 years. It's exciting. They see opportunity. They want to be given a chance to be creative and to make a difference in the lives of both their customers and their teams.

There's the power struggle. One might say that both parties are on equal footing.

I'm going to break it to you. They aren't.

Who do you think I'm going to pick?

It's a fact that it's very easy to start a New Firm today. And customers who want to work differently are looking for other alternatives. So, I believe that ultimately, the retirees are going to have to make an adjustment. There seems to be a common theme that there's no talent. I think there is talent. The talent has not been given an opportunity to lead.

The big firms will get bigger, and there will always be solo practitioners, but the people who have the most to lose are the midsized firms in the middle. The firms with seven to 100 partners who can't agree on how or why they should change.

We need new ways of measuring profitability.

If you look at the 2016 AICPA MAP survey, it explains partner compensation and how firms are profitable overall, using a set of KPIs. It also states that median growth was 5.9 percent.

According to the survey, a firm owner in my gross revenue range states net remaining and owner compensation as $182,294. The biggest issue I have with this survey is that it talks about owner compensation without considering how cloud firm owners are doing it differently.

For example, my firm falls into the $500K - $750K category; however, I have almost no billable hours. Only 30 percent of my time (612 billable hours versus 1307 for a firm my size) would be considered technical in nature, and I have almost no administrative time, as we price and automatically invoice everything up front. I spend my time doing outside things that are not included in my firm compensation. I do spend time doing content creation, marketing, and sales, which allowed our firm to grow 30 percent last year.

NET REMAINING FOR OWNERS AND COMPENSATION					
	2016 Median Net Remaining Per Owner	% Change in Median Net Remaining Per Owner From 2014	2016 Median Owner Compensation	2016 Median Owner Compensation Per Compensated Hour	2016 Median Owner Billing Rate
<$200K	$ 48,111	2.8%	$ 50,000	$ 28.69	$ 150.00
$200K–$500K	$ 128,630	-3.7%	$ 101,422	$ 47.95	$ 165.00
$500K–$750K	$ 182,294	11.2%	$ 142,082	$ 66.87	$ 180.00
$750K–$1.5M	$ 241,817	13.3%	$ 216,667	$ 93.87	$ 200.00
$1.5M–$5M	$ 290,086	-0.9%	$ 254,833	$ 111.11	$ 244.00
$5M–$10M	$ 368,916	-4.0%	$ 323,079	$ 141.16	$ 281.00
>$10M	$ 481,731	4.2%	$ 443,320	$ 175.58	$ 336.00

Source: 2016 MAP Survey - Net Remaining for Owners and Compensation

	<200K	200K<500K	500K<750K	750K<1.5M	1.5M<5M	5M<10M	10M+
Partners/owners (including PT)	1,080	1,300	1,307	1,256	1,178	1,100	1,015
Directors (11+ years' experience)	-	1,280	1,497	1,380	1,233	1,181	1,086
Senior managers (8-10 years' experience)	-	1,516	1,576	1,500	1,398	1,359	1,278
Managers (6–10 years' exp)	-	1,450	1,480	1,502	1,462	1,400	1,364
Senior associates (4–5 years' experience)	-	1,476	1,508	1,507	1,530	1,570	1,500
Associates (1–3 years' experience)	-	1,497	1,404	1,500	1,510	1,545	1,458
New professionals	-	-	1,200	1,441	1,496	1,443	1,349
Paraprofessionals	811	998	1,167	1,290	1,395	1,464	1,438
Interns	-	952	1,048	843	1,200	1,411	1,281
Subcontractors (any experience level)	-	900	1,300	1,291	1,463	1,943	-

Source: 2016 MAP Survey - Utilization

As a New Firm owner, none of the questions they asked in the survey are relevant to my firm style or the way I work. So, I stopped in the middle. I believe the survey is inherently flawed and can't collect the data that indicates what New Firms look like.

While the survey offers some compelling questions, ultimately it cannot measure profitability in New Firm models.

Here's what I mean:

Revenue minus expenses is profit, right? Yes, but . . . to build a long-term sustainable enterprise, firms should look at additional factors, such as:
- Which investments in technology should we make this year to meet future demands?
- What investment in people and processes do we need to make to plan for and create growth?
- Which new services or niches can we invest in to bring to our current and future client base?
- How much should owners be taking out of the business (in terms of compensation of all kinds) versus reinvesting in the future?

All of the above investments negatively affect current-year profits (fees less expenses) but ultimately should lead to higher profitability for the future. Also, when looking at profitability, another key question arises: Is there a cost to owner labor, and, if so, how does that get factored into a profitability model?

What is the cost to owner labor? That is probably the best question—yet one that cannot be answered the old firm model.

Sequel CFO David Boyar says, "For the investment a firm makes in their future, they should also invest time in targeted increased revenue; whilst there is almost no benchmarking on this, owners need to have a targeted revenue figure. If their time is no longer spent on billing, and if it is now spent on content writing, business development, or brand awareness, then a corresponding KPI relates to sales targets."

Armed with sales targets, and an increasing understanding on New Firm profitability (which you can truly only get by doing it, but again, can be targeted) a firm can determine their ROI, RCI, and Yield KPIs. These numbers can determine how much should be taken out from the business.

They also help succession because there is a financial goalpost a prospective buyer can benchmark against.

For example, let's look at a junior partner or manager who has the chance to make two investments. One possibility is working in a firm generating a 24 percent ROI, and the other is buying into a client's business to work in it as a CFO where the ROI is 34 percent. What would the person do? What can you do to make your ROI more attractive?

Why is this model key for the future of firm survival and succession?

Recurring revenue!

When you talk about succession planning, the biggest concern is: Will customers leave the firm?

If they are only annual customers, the probability that they will leave for another CPA firm is high. If you have a subscription-based model, the likelihood of them staying is greater. It's more valuable. Buyers will pay more for a firm that has recurring revenue streams built in. New Firms don't seem to have a problem getting purchased with price tags multiple times their revenue.

The key with the investment of your firm's transformation is in building a recurring revenue model. Subscription-based pricing has inherently more value as a viable business model for continuation.

Hello, valuation CPAs, where have you been?

The subscription model also offers the cash flow opportunity to fuel unparalleled growth. Firm investments should be focused on creating more recurring revenue. It is the ultimate measurement of a current firm's value.

A fun challenge is to identify your current non-recurring revenue and figure out a way to make it keep going. To ask yourself, "What valuable insight can I add to be able to charge for it all year long?" Why did all the individual tax firms add wealth management when Turbo Tax came out?

The two most important questions we should be asking are:
1. What portion of our growth is based in monthly recurring revenue?
2. What does it cost to acquire a recurring revenue customer?

Basically, we need a new MAP survey.

New Firm owners don't do a lot of technical work. They leverage their staff better and use technology effectively. With a better survey, we might have a stronger position as to why going through the difficult work of transforming the actual firm business model is worth it.

Also, there's a statistic that says midsized firm partners make $400K a year. They also work a lot of hours.

Today's generation is not money driven.

If it is possible to make $200K and work 50 percent of the time, is that a reasonable expectation for a New Firm owner? It is and in a much smaller firm.

Is that potentially a door that could open for women to keep them in public accounting?

Could results matter as opposed to just facetime?

Would there be an option for partners to work less and still have the same profitability? If partners can be more profitable by leveraging technology and not utilizing a billable hour methodology, who cares how many hours they work if they bring in revenue? People should be judged on results, not on time spent.

Time & billing is over; here's why

I know you must be tired of me saying this.

But the real reason why I'm able to take on more and focus my energy on expansion is because utilization isn't relevant to my firm.

Utilization needs to go. Scale and capacity make utilization obsolete.

Utilization needs to go. Scale and capacity make utilization obsolete.

Think about it: A typical CPA firm employee is available from 2,100 – 2,200 hours per year. A well-regarded utilization of 80 percent is roughly 1,700 billable hours in a year (42 weeks), and you

> Besides that, measuring utilization operates from a scarcity mindset. The New Firm is all about abundance—and believes that there are more than enough opportunities and time available to get everything done. And do you know why? Technology! Opportunities are not constrained by location. Hello, small local global firm!

haven't done any training, taken vacation, worked on a pursuit, researched anything, or attended a single internal meeting yet. If you utilize technology, your rate will drop exponentially. That's why billing by the hour doesn't work in a technology-driven firm. Everything takes less time because technology can do much of the work humans would typically do.

Besides that, measuring utilization operates from a scarcity mindset. The New Firm is all about abundance—and believes that there are more than enough opportunities and time available to get everything done. And do you know why? Technology! Opportunities are not constrained by location. Hello, small local global firm!

Utilization has been around as long as the billable hour, and worked well when most engagements were a function of maximizing the profit from available human capital.

Measuring utilization and inputs is aligned with the thinking that there are scarce resources and opportunities available (hours, full-time equivalents, customers, projects), and it's in maximizing the utility of these scarce elements that profit is maximized.

If you live in an abundant world where technology is easy to add then it makes more sense to measure value and outputs. Profits are maximized. We are in an age of abundance. Globalization is here.

Want innovation? Get rid of your timesheets!

We talked about this in the culture chapter, but it bears repeating. To have space to innovate and celebrate, I would argue that you need to get rid of your timesheets. For a long time, I've taken the position that I don't keep time but if you choose to keep time that is your prerogative. Now I believe that the longer we stay attached to the timesheet, the further away we are from innovation in our firms. It is the inherent nature of the timesheet that stops innovation and new ideas from happening in a firm. CPAs want to

measure something. Time is not the right thing to measure. When people are required to have timesheets, I've noticed a few things happen:
- An inherent lack of collaboration
- No incentive to look for a more efficient way
- Treating team like an input and not as creative professionals.
- Sticking to a "Can I bill for this mentality?" instead of a customer service mentality
- A lack of engagement re: pricing, and a lack of understanding the firm's actions in relation to firm's ability to earn revenue

Our firm has been without timesheets for 10 years. We have grown and remained profitable and worked significantly less during busy season than other firms. We can manage a successful five-person team (including one remote member) without timesheets. Not having timesheets allows us to work together towards the delighting our customers and delivering on our productized services.

Some New Firms argue that the timesheet is still needed to see if jobs are profitable. To me, that's a shortsighted approach to working in today's new world. If we want consistent innovation, we're going to need to adapt to new technologies, processes, and business models. We're going to need to finally ditch the timesheet. Many businesses today are run without timesheets—why CPAs feel they cannot be run without them is beyond me.

A modernized firm is faster and better.

Technology has allowed my firm to grow. We have developed customized products for our customers. We aim to deliver our services faster, with more efficiency, while bringing more value to the customer. We are focused on their experience, which includes a healthy profit. We do this by automating some of our most basic functions.

All of this is oriented to delivering faster services with less consumption of resources, adding greater value to the customer, and giving talent a better work experience. A firm measuring utilization will disregard these investments, as they are counter to the firm and their personal objective of keeping staff doing billable work, and rewarding self-interest and inefficiency. This is why Ron Baker would say that the timesheet is cancer in a firm.

Product solution-based firms leverage their product/solution across multiple industries or regions. They measure the success of their work in terms of their suite of offerings.

Small firms can choose customer intimacy as a differentiator and price accordingly. Organizationally, they will be categorized by product verticals, and profitability will roll up accordingly. These firms go to market with a message relating to the functional or specific problem they solve, and how their solution differentiates against other competing products or solutions. It's the whole idea of a niche and service lines.

Firms will educate the market on the problem and match their solution to the problem and the persona. As profitability is baked into the price of the product, these firms are oriented around sales metrics, units sold, revenue, and attachment to complimentary products. The customer experience is consistent and reliable. As there is relatively little investment in customers, profitability at the customer level is not as important as sales and marketing targets by region and by product category.

Get comfortable with selling.

But back to one of the main points of this book: We need to sell something other than time. We need to sell an outcome. We need to sell a result. We don't need to sell time anymore. The reason it's so important that we don't sell time anymore is that technology is making time disappear. If you're using something that's completely automated, and you're using electronic downloads, or feeds, things that used to take you two hours now take you two minutes. You're either going to have 25,000 customers, or you're not going to get paid any money, because how do you bill for two minutes?

If you aren't going to measure utilization or sell by it, then why are you tracking time? Just stop measuring it and manage your workload, your team, and your profitability by product.

What our customers want is someone who understands their business, and can provide support and guidance. The ratios and the explanations don't matter in the long run. They want peace of mind. They want to know that you are partnering with them, that you're helping them be the best they can be. I think old-school CPAs get this, but I think they've always been caught in the weeds and haven't had time to really explore this option.

We've always been considered the most trusted advisor. I don't think that's new for CPAs, but I think what's new is to really define what we're selling. We're not just selling customers a tax return, we're just not selling financials, we're selling a connection to improve their business. We understand the data, and we know how all the ratios and calculations work so that they can run their business better. Because that's what they want, they want a result. They don't want to buy a tax return.

> *We're not just selling customers a tax return, we're just not selling financials, we're selling a connection to improve their business.*

It's a lot easier to sell something at a higher price that has tangible value than a tax return. Nobody wants to pay for a tax return.

People switch accountants all the time. Technology is changing and the old firms aren't keeping up. Firms who utilize technology at their core can do more for their clients because they have access to better data faster. It's not that the old CPAs were bad at their jobs, it's just that they weren't using the technology to help them to get them better information. What we hear repeatedly is, "Wow, why didn't my other accountant do this for me?"

Quite honestly, it's a simple answer: time. They didn't have capacity because they were doing so much to just do the technical work, that they couldn't add in the extra advisory on top of it.

But if you're a CPA who can do that, you can help your customers plan and manage the present… and stay relevant in your role at the same time.

You're already a consultant. Now just charge for it. Regularly.

Aside from being the go-to advisor for your customers and staying relevant, you can charge for this knowledge. You can get paid for this because this is really where the value lives. This is where the transformation comes in, and this is what customers want. They're dying for transformational help. We need to get comfortable with these conversations. CPAs always say, "Oh, well, they'll never pay for that."

If you see your small business owners paying for all this coaching, what do you think coaching is?

Coaching *is* advisory.

We have access to the data, we have more knowledge in a customer's file than any outsider, yet we haven't figured out how to take that information and provide services around it, and offer more value to our customers.

To me it's sad, because we should be doing it. And yet, all these other professional consultants are coming in to do it because we don't have the time to do it. Well, if we automate our firms and have technology at our core, then we will have the time to dig into this. Customers pay a lot for advisory, so it's important to get comfortable with advisory. I ask questions that other accountants don't because it's all about getting new and better information.

And frankly, if you don't have those conversations and you don't ask the questions, then it's hard to be helpful. And the data will be more and more accessible as AI and Blockchain evolve. Get in the ring now.

7 Ways to Add Value and Charge For It

- Create accountability. Follow up. Ask a question to a business owner, give them a deadline, and then call them out on the follow-through. This is Coaching 101. Did they do what they said they were going to do? Most small business owners have no one to report to, and they appreciate you taking an interest.
- Set up a tool to measure something. This creates a data point to reflect on or set goals against. Tools add value; there is expectation to pay more when a tool is involved.
- Ask questions independently of the owner. Talk to the team and get unbiased responses. Then ask the owner for their responses. Do the responses align? Is there a problem? How can you help bring their team together?
- Observe, observe, observe.
- Ask questions to truly understand.
- Report written and oral
- Walk alongside, not in front of, the purchaser. This is the hardest for CPAs because they want to deliver all the answers. They key is an outsider's awareness of the situation to help create the solution. Not the ability to solve the problem. Outside-in solutions have a limited shelf life; the solution created with the customer has a better opportunity for success. You want ongoing success because you do not want to be a consultant who is walking away. You will be part of the ongoing solution.

Clients are paying for our expertise and our support. We know that the change is already happening, and the change means that they have new options when it comes to financial decisions. We just need to make sure that as we use new technologies, we do research on them. We need to embrace the new technology. We need to embrace the change so that we can move forward and keep that innovation going in our firms. Because clients will pay for our expertise and support of their transformation, and they'll pay for it more than they'll pay for the data entry or the bookkeeping services. You need to create it as a separate service item and charge according for it. Don't give it away for free.

Remember, Teach Your Team What You Know

It's our communication skills that need improvement. Partners have the skills, but those skills don't get transferred to our lower level employees. Now that everything's in real-time, often our lower level employees are having more critical conversations sooner than the partner. Because of this, we need to figure out how to transfer that knowledge so that we can get our new employees asking the right questions sooner, therefore adding value earlier. More than likely, your newer team members are on the receiving end of more customer responses than you or your other partners, just because of the way the technology has changed and the way work flows through your firm. If we ask more questions, we can then help them get better, and we can get our team members helping the customers better as well. It all comes down to value. Is there an internal tool you can create to help your team ask better questions?

Pre-Billing: Just Say Yes

When you move toward a fixed pricing model the easiest thing to do is pre-bill. It gives you the ability to grow because it allows you to increase your capacity before the work comes in. With the extra capacity you can make plans, get organized, and facilitate change in your organization.

One of the biggest problems for old-school firms is that their staffing never matches their needs and it burns out existing staff. If you pre-bill and use subscription-based pricing, it's much easier to manage capacity. I would even argue that the firms who have succeeded in growing have created the capacity before the growth. This is a completely new way of thinking for a firm. Will your customer accept a pre-bill? Absolutely, because it is a fixed price.

But remember, not every customer is the right match for your firm. Not every person who comes in your firm needs to become a customer. That's OK. Accept it.

CHAPTER 8
Join the Radical Movement

Get Going!

You've read my Beyond Radical approach.

Are you exhausted or energized? If you know me, you know that I can't wait to help you get started on your journey.

Are you ready to get started?

Is this book the way to a Utopian Firm?

I think it is.

Remember, Utopian includes happiness as a factor. If our firms don't include happiness, I think we need to rethink what we are doing.

Hopefully this roadmap will get you moving.

Undergoing this transformation can only make us better professionals for our customers. The transformation will also be incredible for our employees and partners. Sometimes I think an outside catalyst is helpful to persuade us to move forward . . . even though we know our firms need to start this journey today.

Maybe even yesterday.

Anticipatory Organization

Al DeLeon, founding partner of DeLeon and Stang in Virginia and Maryland, has introduced the Anticipatory Organization model to their firm. What does that mean exactly?

As an anticipatory organization, DeLeon & Stang assists clients in recognizing hard and soft trends that could be influencing their business. By identifying these trends through a "flash forward" approach and the use of technology, DeLeon & Stang can help business owners (including themselves) take advantage of opportunities and drive innovation.

This model was co-created with the Maryland Association of CPAs' Tom Hood and futurist Daniel Burrus. I was able to catch up with DeLeon and hear how this approach has impacted their firm.

First, he gave me a little history about his firm: "We are 32 years old; our gross revenue right now is about $7.5 million, and we have about 45 people. We have two offices and we're about to open a third. We are a large local firm. We do all sort of accounting work, mostly financial statement audits, reviews, comps, and outsourced CFO. We have an investment advisory subsidiary and a pretty big tax department; we do a lot of individual tax and business tax.

JP: **Okay, I know that you and your firm went through Tom Hood's Anticipatory CPA Program.**

AD: We did.

JP: **Can you tell us a little about why you chose to go through the program, and then how you've seen it change your firm?**

AD: Well, we went through it because we love Tom. Tom introduced it to us; he does our strategic planning retreat, has done so now for probably 10 years, and we really liked the idea. We put our whole staff through the training. We actually have an Anticipatory Organization committee within the firm, where we try to encourage people to use this anticipatory forward-thinking concept with our clients. When [our employees] have a story to tell, we publicize them and try to keep the energy going.

For the most part we find clients are pretty receptive to the idea. It's a little hard for some of them to get their head around it because they're in the weeds doing whatever they do every day. It's very hard to get people to step back and think about what it's going to be like in the future and what do I need to do now?

But we're using it within our firm to try to plan where we're going from a strategic standpoint. For example, we're very concerned about the automation of the basic accounting services and even tax services that could be coming down the pipe. How do we adjust our services to provide value add so that we don't get Uber-ized, so to speak, with the technology changes that are coming along?

JP: **Do you think that your younger CPAs, or people who are newer to the profession, have liked this approach and have experienced it as relevant to them?**

AD: Oh yeah, absolutely. They like it probably more than the more seasoned folks because they see the technology stuff as being cool, and they like seeing all the different technologies that are available these days. So, they resonate pretty well with that.

We're not really generating a lot of engagements from the anticipatory, it's more using it to serve the clients, get the clients thinking about what they need to do, especially around succession planning. There are so many businesses that need succession planning these days. So, that was actually the area that we focused on with respect to anticipatory organizations ... trying to help clients develop a succession plan and figure out what the business is going to look like in 10 years. Who's going to be running it? What kind of competition are they going to be facing? What kind of technologies could disrupt them? That kind of stuff.

JP: **Many CPAs think that they already are proactive. What's the difference between being proactive and being anticipatory?**

AD: It's just a different way of looking at it. It's still proactive, but proactive in the sense that it's trying to help the client look at his business and his industry, and the technology changes that are taking place, and think about strategic planning from the perspective of: What is the competition going to be doing? What is it going to look like in five or 10 years, or even faster? That's the other thing too, some of this stuff happens very fast.

I'll give you an example. One of our clients is [a] taxi credit union in New York City. All they do is make taxi medallion loans, for years, and it's a very profitable credit union. All their loans are 100 percent collateralized by taxi medallions that had a solid market that would never go down ... until Uber.

They were taken over; they're being [placed under conservatorship] because their loan losses are so high. They had a $28 million loss last year; we had to give them a going concern opinion. And many times we suggested to them, "Look, you need to try to think about diversifying your loan portfolio, get into auto loans, expand your field of membership, get into mortgages." They never wanted to do it because they were doing so great with taxi medallion loans, they thought, "Well, why should we get involved in other loan products that are less profitable and more risky?"

That was even before we got into the anticipatory organization stuff. But that is an example of a client that didn't [take our advice]. We didn't know that Uber was coming along, but we said, "There's a lot of value in diversifying." And they didn't do it, and now they're basically going out of business.

JP: **Do you think that if CPAs don't become anticipatory, like all CPAs as the profession, that we risk losing relevance to our client base?**

AD: I don't know. There's always going to be need for CPAs to do the basic compliance work and the tax returns and things like that; it's really no different than the way it's been for 100 years, things always change, just that now it's changing fast.

We've always been pretty innovative anyway, but what it's done is help us think that we have to move faster and think about things that we might not have otherwise thought about.

For example, just take outsourced accounting. We worked on that a number of years ago, built up a department that does that kind of work, and we started using technology so we could do the work virtually. We started using things like Bill.com so that clients could pay electronically, put QuickBooks on a secure server, all that kind of stuff.

That was using technology. What we're doing now is, we're thinking about how we're going to deal with the situation that nobody needs us to post the transactions anymore, these transactions are going to get posted automatically. The low end of that work is going to be all automatic. So that's what we're thinking about now, how are we going to deal with that? How are we going to help clients use that efficiently? Which would hopefully give us time to help them at a high-end level.

The strategic planning meetings that we do every year help, and as I said, Tom helps us facilitate it. So really, throughout the organization, we're pretty much all on the same page. We're aligned; we've always had good alignment from the partners. But Tom definitely helps us understand that the pace of change is fast and we have to continue to learn and we have to continue to try to keep up and anticipate what could be coming down the road.

JP: **When you hear about other firms that don't embrace innovation and technology and change, do you have any suggestions for them? Or helpful tips for someone who wants to create change but is having a problem at the partner level to get buy-in?**

AD: Wake up. I do think strategic planning is important, and the way we do it here is we use everybody at the firm.

We end up with half a dozen big initiatives that we want to work on, bold steps. So then there's an internal committee for each one and they work on it throughout the year, reporting on it throughout the year. Then we get back for the next year's session and we say, "Okay, how did we do?" We don't always get everything done, of course, but nobody does.

That's really how we do that. As I said, it's kind of built into our culture here, so getting alignment and agreement from the partners is not a problem.

I had a guy the other day, he goes, "What do you think about this cloud computing idea?" I'm like, "Holy, mackerel! He's just thinking about that now?"

So, you know, what they need is a heavy dose of Tom Hood.

We can't fear change. Our only choice is to learn what's going on, to learn about the bots that are coming our way. It's our job to learn about the technology so that we can help our customers move through it. If we don't, my biggest fear is that we're going to risk losing relevancy.

I truly believe that if we don't move with the digital transformation, we're going to go away, and all the consultants are going to come in and step in our place, and we're going to lose our seat at the table. I'm not saying this to freak everyone out, but we have to realize that we really need to not fear change, and to keep moving, and to keep learning. We have everything to do it right at our fingertips.

Innovation, agile, product management, becoming anticipatory, and diversity and inclusion are not in your typical CPA practice management books. Because they are not typical issues. Some might even call them Beyond Radical.

We know our firms don't feel contemporary anymore, and they haven't felt right for a while. We know we are looking for a silver bullet to take us into the unknown future. Our movement is made of the innovators, and we are finding big wins and success in our new methodologies of running New Firms differently. Why not join us in our journey? We now have proven it can be successful.

If there's one thing you walk away with in reading this book, let it be this: CPAs, it's up to you to lead in your firms.

It's up to you to illustrate what innovation means in the context of practice management.

The economy is increasingly motivated by innovation that is led by business. As a business owner's most trusted advisor, we do a shockingly poor job at creating ongoing, consistent opportunities for innovations in our firms. How are we modeling our cutting-edge knowledge and insight? Many CPAs aren't, and instead are getting blown away by the competition. Core transformation is where the Radical CPA model lives.

Remember the story of Netflix. Anthony points to the subscription-based company as an example of how they continued to reinvent themselves to stay cutting edge. They moved away from sending DVDs through the mail to streaming video content via the Web. They transitioned from just distributing other entertainment content to creating their own. Netflix is a remarkable example of how tuning into customer preferences informs new offerings and how it stays ahead of the curve. Wouldn't you say the Radical CPAs have done this with accounting firms? I would.

I believe operating our firms with core technology principles that have innovation, adaptation, and product management built into their core is what a Utopian CPA firm will resemble. This is the new strategic model. I'm sure there are parts we still don't know as well.

This strategic model is our challenge. It's the structure of how we build the New Firm 2.0. This is beyond what we already know. And remember what Anthony wrote, "Executed successfully, strategic transformation reinvigorates a company's growth engine. Poor execution leads naysayers to pounce and complain that a company should have 'stuck to its knitting.'"

I leave you with a few questions:

How much time and money are you willing to invest in your transformation?

What legacy beliefs are holding you back?

And will you join me?

Thank Yous, Thoughts, and Ramblings:

I so love the professionals who challenge me to up my game. Sometimes it's hard being a Radical with extreme ideas, but along the way, I have met some incredible professionals who helped me to grow by accepting and challenging my beliefs. The professionals who are innovative at their core and understand me. They seem to be drawn to me. They have experience and wisdom to move my thinking to a higher level. I didn't really understand that in my younger days, and often felt it was "me against them." I am so thankful for them and their ongoing feedback.

The biggest takeaway for me in writing this second book was really getting to know and understand larger firm perspectives. For that I am most thankful. And the most exciting thing is seeing the bubbles of innovation starting to form and transform them.

This book began in a coffee shop in New York, in November 2016, when Rick Telberg and I were talking about the evolution of ideas, and I said that I was bored with *The Radical CPA* content. I needed something new to evolve me. I guess that's why they say I'm a visionary… I just think I get bored quickly. So, it was decided. I thought I had enough content to write a new book. And because I could, I would write during tax season. I talked to Liz Gold, who helps me create most of my content, and she was on board. Then I jumped on a plane that following January for a writers' retreat with best-selling authors Michael Port and Mike Michalowicz. There, I realized that I would write specifically for a midsized firm owner. They helped me as I refined my outline and my audience. And Mike makes a mean margarita. It was great to spend a few days with people who are writing books, a truly inspiring weekend. And then I wrote, and wrote, and refined, and wrote some more. This book is nothing like the first, and yet it amazes me how they both are mine. Like when you have kids, they are yours—each one is so different yet so amazing. I got critical feedback to make it the best it could be. And now, I can say I've written two books. I'm an author!

Shout-outs…

My husband Chris. Thank you for being my partner in everything. There is no way I could be as successful as I am without you at my side. And for

Chapter 6 in *The Radical CPA: New Rules for a Future-Ready Firm*. You are a process master!

Alex, my right hand and left foot, and now a principal in New Vision CPA Group. We built this New Firm together, I just talk a lot more. I promise to sign and inscribe your copy!

Dad, I'm happy to carry on the family values you instilled when you founded the firm. Our core is unstoppable. Retirement looks good on you. Mom, thank you for always listening; I wonder how many CEOs still ask their moms for their opinion.

Kayleigh Padar, my superstar writer, who just happens to be my college-bound daughter. She wrote these case studies:

> *New Thinking From the Group Up: An Interview with Josh Zweig of LiveCA LLP*
>
> *Karbon is Building a Practice Management Platform on Steroids: An Interview with Cofounder Ian Vacin*
>
> *"If You're Not Disrupting, You're Not Doing it Right:" An Interview with Dean Quiambao of Armanino LLP*
>
> *Capitalizing on Capacity: An Interview with Father/Son Team Bernard N. Ackerman, CPA/PFS, CFP, CGMA, CDFA and Jason L. Ackerman CPA, CFP, CGMA of BNA CPA*
>
> *Revolutionizing HR: An Interview with Brad Self of Clark Schaefer Hackett*
>
> *A Platform for Practice Management: An Interview With Chris Hooper of Accodex*

Jimmy Padar, my teenage son, who is constantly judging my lack of motherhood responsibilities. I'm really working toward a rating of 10. This shout-out should get me to at least an eight.

Liz Gold, thank you for all you do with my content. Pushing it further, editor extraordinaire, and challenging my thinking. I love that we can agree to disagree and still have such a good relationship.

Maggie, where will wealth management be next year? I can't wait to find out.

Sheryl and Madeline (Team New Vision) . . . it's only just begun; I'm glad you are along for the ride.

For all my technology partners, keep innovating so we can remain relevant. The profession can't do this without you.

Last. But not least. 1st Global. Excited to be on this journey with you.

About CPA Trendlines

From Success to Significance: The Radical CPA Guide is published by CPA Trendlines, an imprint of Bay Street Group LLC.

CPA Trendlines provides actionable intelligence to help tax, accounting and finance professionals advance their firms and their careers at http://cpatrendlines.com

Join CPA Trendlines as a PRO Member

Get full site-wide access to exclusive content, insights and research, plus join a community of forward-thinking colleagues and get great offers and discounts on other CPA Trendlines products and services, http://cpaclick.com/pro-upgrade

Find more products and services like this from CPA Trendlines at store.cpatrendlines.com

- What Really Makes CPA Firms Profitable?
- The Rosenberg MAP Survey: The Leading Annual National Study of CPA Firm Statistics
- The CPA Trendlines Succession Institute
- The CPA Trendlines Pathfinder Series for Practice Owners
- The Client Service Idea Book
- Accountant's Accelerator
- The Accountant's (Bad) Joke Book
- The 90-Day Marketing Plan for CPA Firms
- The 30:30 Training Method
- Tax Season Opportunity Guide
- Strategic Planning and Goal Setting for Results
- Sponsoring Women: What Men Need to Know

- Quantum of Paperless: The Partners Guide to Accounting Firm Optimization
- Professional Services Marketing 3.0
- Passport to Partnership
- Leadership at its Strongest
- Implementing Fee Increases
- How to Review Tax Returns
- How to Operate a Compensation Committee
- How to Engage Partners in the Firm's Future
- How to Create the Roadmap for Your Firm's Growth
- How to Bring in New Partners
- How CPA Firms Work: The Business of Public Accounting
- Guide to Planning the Firm Retreat
- Effective Partner Relations and Communications
- Creating the Effective Partnership: Two-Volume Package
- CPA Firm Succession Planning: A Perfect Storm
- CPA Firm Partner Retirement / Buyout Plans
- CPA Firm Mergers: Your Complete Guide CPA Firm Management & Governance
- Accounting Marketing 101 Partners
- Accounting Firm Operations and Technology Survey
- 101 Questions and Answers: Managing an Accounting Practice
- Price it Right
- The Complete Guide to Marketing for Tax & Accounting Firms

Made in the USA
San Bernardino, CA
08 April 2018